With Heads Held High

Legacy of My Southern Parents

Odessa Walker Hooker

Dear Ossie,
Prayer is a powerful privilege to
practice.

Love + prayers,
Odessa
3/12/2004

Densmore Reid Publications
Richmond Indiana

With Heads Held High:
Legacy Of My Southern Parents
Copyright ©2003
By Odessa Walker Hooker

Published by
Densmore Reid Publications
67 South 24th Street, Richmond, IN 47374

ISBN 0-9700827-3-8

Cover Art by
Stephen Geddes

Commissioned for the 50th Wedding Anniversary
of Anderson and Pauline Walker
Used with permission

Published by arrangement with Prinit Press, Richmond, Indiana
Manufactured in the United States of America on acid-free paper

Except the Lord build the house,

they labor in vain that build it:...

Lo, children are a heritage of the Lord:

and the fruit of the womb is His reward.

As arrows are in the hand of a mighty man;

so are children of the youth.

Happy is the man that hath his quiver full of them:

they shall not be ashamed,

but they shall speak with the enemies in the gate.

Psalm 127:1,3-5 (KJV)

This book is dedicated to the Glory of God in loving memory and gratitude to my parents who, with God's help did a superb job of rearing nine children, and to dedicated teachers who helped my siblings and me become contributing citizens.

Acknowledgements

My special thanks to all the people who had a hand in making this work a success:

- Delta Kappa Gamma Society International for scholarship help
- Dr. Daryl and Anne Rose Greene, incredible editors and publishers
- Pearline W. Singletary, constant companion, helper and encourager
- Pastor Mendle Adams, my encouraging pastor who introduced me to the editors/publishers, and who took time to read the manuscript and write an endorsement
- Mary Jane Y. Kaufman, Ph.D. encourager, who read and edited the manuscript and wrote an endorsement
- Dr. Peter Magolda who read the original and the revised manuscript, and wrote an endorsement
- All family members who sent contributions for the manuscript:
  Pearline Walker Singletary
  Anderson Walker, Jr.
  Oreatha Walker Ensley
  Mose Ensley, Jr.
  Andrea Walker Ice
  Kenneth O'Neal Walker
  George Walker
  Edna Hill
  Opral Walker Davis
  Michael Holloway
  Melanie Hooker Johnson
  Margaret Pauline Hooker
  Darrell Walker Hooker
  Adam Mattocks
- Edwenia Rutledge who used her computer skills to produce the genealogies and the pictures
- Rubye Glenn who helped with the whole project and traveled with me
- The committee who planned and executed the book release reception:

Pearline W. Singletary	Melanie Hooker Johnson
Mary Jane Kaufman	Kathleen Dupree
Rubye Glenn	Andrea W. Ice

IV

Contents

Part One: Recollections Of My Parents and Family, 1927-1951

Foreword

I decided to get involved in helping Odessa Walker Hooker publish this book because Odessa is a hero. Not a perfect fairy tale figure, but a real flesh and blood woman who overcame the obstacles of poverty and racism to raise her family and become an award winning educator.

Odessa's life and accomplishments first came to public attention in 1993, when she was recognized as The Cincinnati Enquirer Woman of the Year. In 2001 she received national recognition when she was given the Excellence In Teaching Award from the United Church of Christ General Synod. In this book, she describes her journey from growing up in a shack in southern Georgia to the top of the teaching profession.

Odessa attributes her success to the fact that she built her life on the legacy of her poor Southern parents and their example of faith, self sacrifice, family commitment, and hard work. In this book she seeks to honor their life and the gifts they have given her.

Odessa was the first of nine children born to Anderson and Pauline Walker, growing up in Georgia under the Jim Crow laws of the 1930's. Part of the Walker legacy was that they taught their children to walk with heads held high. When spoken to by whites, blacks were expected to bow their heads and look down. But Anderson Walker did not teach Odessa to act in this subservient and demeaning manner. He taught her to walk with her head up, her eyes alert to what was going on around her, and to look adults in the eye when spoken to, whether they were black or white. He taught her to act like a person who had intelligence, integrity and dignity. Odessa grew up expecting that she could and would make her mark in the world.

I have been moved by the details of Odessa's story. I am honored to invite you to step into her life and experience what it took for her to become a true American hero.

Dr. Daryl C. Greene
Editor, Densmore Reid Publications

Preface

I have spent my adult life dispelling a prevailing myth in the black community; namely, blacks are inferior. They are doomed to failure because they lack motivation, education, and know how to achieve the American Dream. Hogwash! Baloney! We are beneficiaries of a gift much greater than the "American Dream." Our Creator endows us with the gifts of love, intelligence, sincere caring for each other, and a willingness to share whatever resources we possess.

Despite this society's efforts to destroy the Black family, we are survivors! Many black families have overcome the destructive obstacles that have been placed in our path. We have done so because our Creator endows us with gifts of faith, perseverance in adversity, and hearts of compassion.

There is no waste in God's economy. There is also no limit to His abilities. The idea for this book evolved from the realization that by God's grace my parents defeated the odds against a successful marriage, and the successful rearing of nine children. They also sacrificed to ensure that six of their children received a college education. At the Walker-Hill Family Reunion in 1980, Daddy made this statement: "Mr. Gentlemen (an expression he used to indicate seriousness of his comments), look around this room! My wife and I have reared nine heads of children, thirty-two grandchildren, and sixteen great-grandchildren. You don't see one cigarette, one alcoholic drink, and I can tell you, I have never had one to go to jail!" Wow! What a legacy!

Thankfully, all of us children were born sound of mind and body. Without the benefit of health insurance, we grew up mostly healthy. Mama and Daddy lacked lucrative opportunities. As head of the household, Daddy worked menial jobs to allow Mama to stay home with the children; often, he worked two or three jobs.

At the same time, Daddy and Mama did not think of themselves as model parents, yet their parenting can teach modern couples wisdom about sustaining strong marriages. Daddy and Mama took their roles as parents seriously. Mama believed that Daddy should be the head of the family, and he readily assumed that role. She allowed him to make the major decisions, yet she always contributed her ideas. In the face of danger, when Daddy was absent, she exhibited unusual bravery. Once a snake came into the house through the chimney. One of the children rushed to tell Mama that a snake was crawling up the leg of Betty's bed. Mama rushed into the room, grabbed the snake by the tail, carried it through the kitchen, and threw it out the door! Then she fainted!

On another occasion Mama demonstrated her bravery when Daddy was absent and suddenly a storm came up. Mama was always respectful of severe weather. During thunderstorms we were instructed to sit still and do nothing. We could not read a book or even talk to each other. This particular storm was accompanied by high winds, so powerful that the front door blew open. I watched as my Mama with unusual strength pushed the door shut and held it. She used a quilt to blunt the rain that was blowing into the house. Mama held that door shut with her body as she prayed fervently for God's help. Almost as suddenly as it had started, the storm subsided. Mama released the door, then began to dry the floor and restore order.

Mama also interpreted Daddy's character to us by her respectful actions toward him and comments about him. On more than one occasion she said to us, "If your daddy had been educated, he'd have been this country's first black president." I believed her.

Our parents cooperated with God's plan for building healthy families! We are the beneficiaries of their intelligence and work ethic. Daddy demonstrated his belief in God's command that parents should teach their children about God. He didn't *send* us Anderson Walker *accompanied* his children to Sunday school and church every week. He regularly participated in church matters. Early in our lives we came to understand that we were to be active in church, including serving wherever we could, and paying our tithes. He gave the offering to us until we began to earn money to pay our own. Mama and Daddy parented day-by-day as best they could. But they explicitly believed in god's promises, and, to the best of their abilities, acted on them. Their story bears recording, especially in this age of broken homes and dysfunctional families. I pray that the generations to follow in our family will emulate Daddy's and Mama's parenting style, and continue to perpetuate the legacy of this remarkable poor, Southern African American couple.

XII

Years later, when my children's daddy left us, the nay-sayers predicted that I would not be able to maintain my family. But, to gain strength, I recalled how Daddy and Mama had been successful, and mimicked their approach to parenting. There were times when I had no job, no money, no food in the refrigerator, and five hungry mouths to feed, not including my own. Without the loving support of my extended family we would not have made it. Likewise with the aid of neighbors and friends we would not have survived or gone on to be successful. Such people were often the agents of God's miracles. I relied on my college education, and became an award-winning educator in Cincinnati. For many years, I prayerfully solo parented my five children while working full time. I passed on the legacy of my parents and saw to it that my children also received college degrees. As an educator I never encountered a child I couldn't teach. All children can learn but not all learn in the same way. As a teacher, I was always delighted to see Black children achieve when given an opportunity and a challenge.

I wrote this book to give future generations hope. My desire is to encourage the reader to put his or her faith in the help of Almighty God, for as the reader will soon discover, it is by His miracles that I survived and became successful beyond my wildest expectations.

The book is divided into three parts: (1) my recollections of my parents and family; (2) my personal story as wife, parent, and educator; and, (3) recollections about Mama and Daddy contributed by other family members.

It is my prayer that readers of my story will be inspired to share their stories with their families and others.

Odessa Walker Hooker

Descendants of James T. Walker (1 of 10)

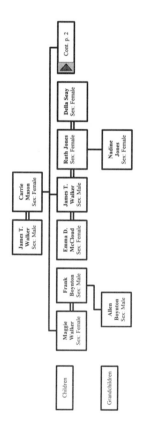

Cont. p. 2

Descendants of James T. Walker (2 of 10)

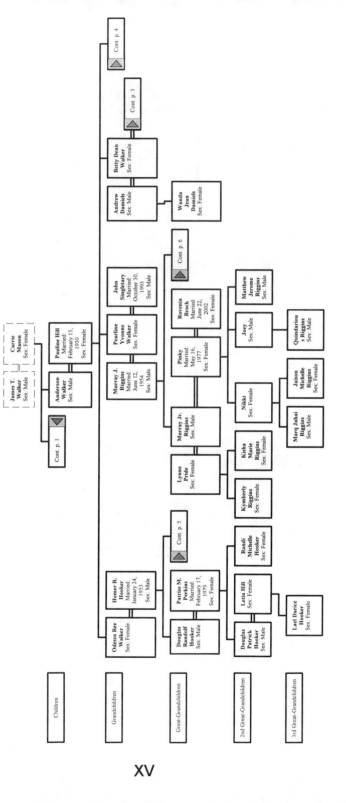

Cont. p. 4
Cont. p. 3
Cont. p. 1
Cont. p. 5
Cont. p. 6

Children

Grandchildren

Great-Grandchildren

2nd Great-Grandchildren

3rd Great-Grandchildren

James T. Walker Sex: Male — **Carrie Mason** Sex: Female

Pauline Hill Married: February 15, 1930 Sex: Female

Anderson Walker Sex: Male

Andrew Daniels Sex: Male

Betty Dean Walker Sex: Female

Wanda Jean Daniels Sex: Female

Murray J. Riggins Married: June 12, 1954 Sex: Male

Pearline Yvonne Walker Sex: Female

John Singletary Married: October 30, 1993 Sex: Male

Lynne Pride Sex: Female

Murray Jr. Riggins Sex: Male

Pinky Married: May 16, 1977 Sex: Female

Rovenia Brock Married: June 22, 2002 Sex: Female

Kymberly Riggins Sex: Female

Kisha Marie Riggins Sex: Female

Nikki Sex: Female

Joey Sex: Male

Matthew Jerome Riggins Sex: Male

Marq Jahai Riggins Sex: Male

Jaison Michelle Riggins Sex: Female

Quindarius Riggins Sex: Male

Odessa Ree Walker Sex: Female

Homer R. Hooker Married: January 24, 1953 Sex: Male

Douglas Randolf Hooker Sex: Male

Patrise M. Perkins Married: February 17, 1979 Sex: Female

Douglas Patrick Hooker Sex: Male

Letia Hill Hooker Sex: Female

Randi Michelle Hooker Sex: Female

Lael Darice Hooker Sex: Female

XV

Descendants of James T. Walker (3 of 10)

Great-Grandchildren

2nd Great-Grandchildren

Hollis B. Holloway Married April 29, 1954 Sex: Male	Betty Dean Walker Sex: Female

Cont. p. 2

Great-Grandchildren level:
- Beverly Holloway — Sex: Female
- Samuel W. Swain — Sex: Male
- Kimberly Holloway — Sex: Female
- John Priester — Sex: Male
- Letitia Denise Holloway — Sex: Female
- Malcolm Martin — Sex: Male
- Maria Babrow — Sex: Female
- Michael Andre Holloway — Sex: Male
- Susan Pinkerton — Sex: Female
- Hollis Jr. Holloway — Sex: Male
- Gail Clark — Sex: Female
- Wayne Jerome Holloway — Sex: Male
- Charlene Ward — Sex: Female

2nd Great-Grandchildren level:
- Abrica Toyelle Swain — Sex: Female
- Samuel W. Jr Swain — Sex: Male
- Jeremy O'cean Priester — Sex: Male
- Sada Monique Priester — Sex: Female
- Chassidy Yvonne Martin — Sex: Female
- Malisha Martin — Sex: Female
- Michael Andre Jr. Holloway — Sex: Male
- Monique Maria Holloway — Sex: Female
- Zoe Holloway — Sex: Female
- Hollisia Nicloe Holloway — Sex: Female
- Daphney Yvette Holloway — Sex: Female
- Melissa Holloway — Sex: Female

XVI

Descendants of James T. Walker (4 of 10)

Cont. p. 7

Anderson Walker
Sex: Male
Married: February 15, 1930
Pauline Hill
Sex: Female

Cont. p. 2

Grandchildren

Claire Soso
Sex: Female

Anderson Jr. Walker
Sex: Male

Ida Mae Roberts
Sex: Female

Yuba Albert
Married: October 27, 1962
Sex: Female

Lillie Martin
Sex: Female

Freddie James Walker
Sex: Male

Opral D. Foster
Married: September 14, 1968
Sex: Female

Great-Grandchildren

Darian Jones Walker
Sex: Male

Frances Roberts Walker
Sex: Female

Fazal Kader Chowdhury
Sex: Male

Parthy Jo Walker
Sex: Female

Cookie
Sex: Female

Angeline Walker
Sex: Female

Warren Harris
Married: July 29, 1998
Sex: Male

Fredricka Pauline Walker
Sex: Female

Freddie James Jr. Walker
Sex: Male

2nd Great-Grandchildren

Danielle Harris
Sex: Female

Naomi Harris
Sex: Female

XVII

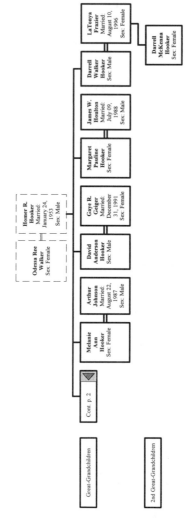

Descendants of James T. Walker (6 of 10)

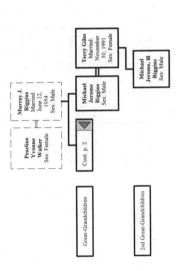

Cont. p. 2

Great-Grandchildren

2nd Great-Grandchildren

XIX

Descendants of James T. Walker (7 of 10)

Cont. p. 8

Anderson Walker
Sex: Male

Pauline Hill
Married: February 15, 1930
Sex: Female

Oreatha LaVerne Walker
Sex: Female

Mose M. Ensley
Sex: Male

Andrea Christine Walker
Sex: Female

Sherrod E. Ice
Married: January 26, 1968
Sex: Male

Kenneth O'Neal Walker
Sex: Male

Beverly DeBrie
Married: February 14, 1981
Sex: Female

Cont. p. 4

Allison Ensley
Sex: Female

Dedrick Ensley
Sex: Male

Kim Ensley
Sex: Female

Cont. p. 9

Michelle Yvette Ice
Sex: Female

Cedric Halyard
Married: March 14, 1991
Sex: Male

Cont. p. 10

Davna Coney Walker
Sex: Male

Kimberly Edwards Walker
Sex: Female

Michelle Knighton Walker
Sex: Female

Aisha Cherise Walker
Sex: Female

Jordan Anderson Walker
Sex: Male

Christian Dane Halyard
Sex: Male

Cedria Alexis Halyard
Sex: Female

Chandler Michelle Halyard
Sex: Female

Grandchildren

Great-Grandchildren

2nd Great-Grandchildren

XX

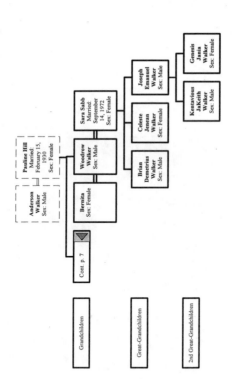

Descendants of James T. Walker (8 of 10)

Cont. p. 7

Anderson Walker
Sex: Male

Pauline Hill
Married: February 15, 1930
Sex: Female

Bernita
Sex: Female

Woodrow Walker
Sex: Male

Sara Sabb
Married: September 14, 1972
Sex: Female

Brian Demetrius Walker
Sex: Male

Celeste Jenean Walker
Sex: Female

Joseph Emanuel Walker
Sex: Male

Kentavious JaKeith Walker
Sex: Male

Genesis Jania Walker
Sex: Female

Grandchildren

Great-Grandchildren

2nd Great-Grandchildren

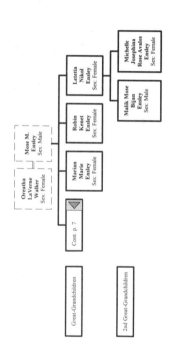

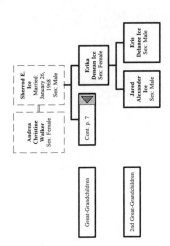

Great-Grandchildren

2nd Great-Grandchildren

Descendants of George Washington Hill (1 of 3)

Virginia Shafe

George W Hill 1865 - 1947 — Solome 1887 -

Geneie Hill — Valley Mouser

Elizabeth Lizzie Hill 1899 - 1980 — Allen Smith 1895 - 1973

Cont. p. 2

Cont. p. 3

Robert Wright — Bertha Smith 1917 - — Charles Coleman

Charles Jr Coleman

Jimmie Elsworth Smith 1938 - 1982

Kim Smith

Elnou Smith

Elizabeth Maxine Smith 1940 -

Angel Yvette Roach — Thompson

Andre Thompson

Robert Thompson

Roach

Ronica Michelle Roach — Moore

Sheila Moore

Nicole Moore

Keiugh Lamont Moore

Britany Angie Moore

Leva Hill 1919 -

Jimmy Smith 1918 -

Frank Jr Delberry 1959 -

Bryant

Taft Delberry Bryant 1970s

Ronald Bryant 1970s

Destiny Kelly Bryant 1985 -

Sabrina Delberry 1962 -

Satyn Delberry 1977 -

Durfer

Frank Delberry

Regina Delberry 1963 -

Maurice Harris Delberry 1978 -

Gertrude Smith 1942 -

Leva Shawn Delberry 1965 -

Marcus Delberry 1982 -

Oliver

Toby Eugene Smith 1943 - 1993

Allen Delberry 1967 -

Tiera U Whitener 1986 -

Rodney Whitener

Rodney Jr Whitener 1988 -

Morgan P Whitener 1989 -

Rachel

Allen II Smith 1947 -

Christina Smith

Jaki Smith

Michael wade Smith 1962 -

Patricia

Michael Jr Smith

Ashley Smith

Children

Grandchildren

Great-Grandchildren

2nd Great-Grandchildren

3rd Great-Grandchildren

XXIV

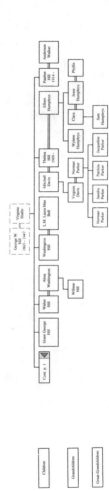

Children

Grandchildren

Great-Grandchildren

Descendants of George Washington Hill (3 of 3)

George W
Hill
1865 - 1947

Sailome
1887 -

Cont. p. 1

| Children | Grandchildren | Great-Grandchildren | 2nd Great-Grandchildren |

Laurey
Hill

Minnie
Cameron

Eugene
Hill

Lial
Merriweather

Solome Bell
Hill

Ulysses
Hankerson

David
Cox

Odessa
Hill
1926 -

Robert
Shephard

Jessie Pearl
Hill
1931 -

Richard
Allen

Larry
Hill

Phyllis
Appleton

Devis
Chamberlin

Eugene Jr
Hill

Donna
Hill

Bernice
Hankerson

Larry
Wiggins

Ulysses
Hankerson

Rudry

Ulysses Jr
Hankerson
1945 -

Mercedes

Patricia
Cox
1943 -

Ronald
Berry

David
Cox
1944 -

Donald
De Vraux

Charles Danny
De Vraux
1950 -

Rene
Johnson

Jennifer
De Vraux
1952 -

Dwayne
Bailey
1953 -

Nicey
Allen
1955 -

Willie II
Stephens

Shawn
Hill

Larry Jr
Wiggins

Liliana
Perez

Valerie
Wiggins

Angela
Wiggins

Douglas
Wiggins

Terry
Washington

Lynette
Hankerson

Isaiah
Walton

Josep
Devis
1983 -

De A.
Berry

Troy David
Berry

Rhoniel Patrise
Berry

Rhonda
Berry

Darren
DuBois

Rhonside Tasha
Berry
1983 -

Michael
Lymon

Tanya
De Vraux

Nakara
Stephens

Leslie Barnes
Stephens

Willie III
Stephens

Caleb
Stephens

Olivia
Wiggins
1998 -

Vanessa
Wiggins
2000 -

Darren II
DuBois

Darren II
DuBois

Tasha
Lymon

Aurianna
Lymon

Descendants of Willis Sr Hill (1 of 5)

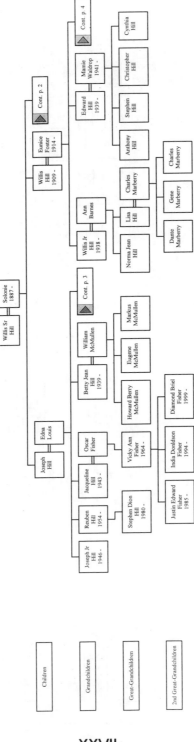

Children

Grandchildren

Great-Grandchildren

2nd Great-Grandchildren

XXVII

Descendants of Willis Sr Hill (2 of 5)

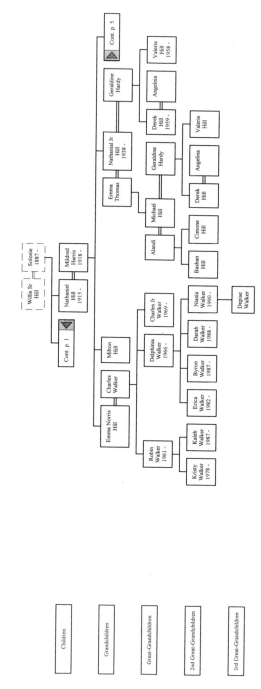

Children

Grandchildren

Great-Grandchildren

2nd Great-Grandchildren

3rd Great-Grandchildren

Descendants of Willis Sr Hill (3 of 5)

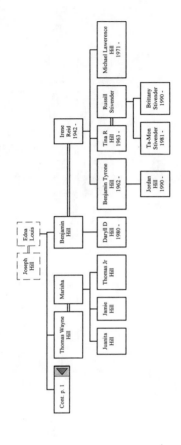

Cont. p. 1

Joseph Hill — Edna Louis

Thomas Wayne Hill — Marisha

Benjamin Hill — Irene Reid 1942 -

Juanita Hill
Jamie Hill
Thomas Jr Hill

Daryll D Hill 1980 -

Benjamin Tyrone Hill 1962 -
Jordan Hill 1990 -

Tina R Hill 1963 - — Russill Stivender
Ta-Mon Stivender 1981 -
Brittany Stivender 1990 -

Michael Lawerence Hill 1971 -

Grandchildren

Great-Grandchildren

2nd Great-Grandchildren

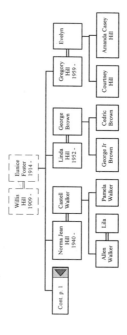

Willis
Hill
1909 -

Eunice
Foster
1914 -

Cont. p. 1

Norma Jean
Hill
1940 -

Castell
Walker

Linda
Hill
1952 -

George
Brown

Gregory
Hill
1959 -

Evelyn

Allen
Walker

Lila

Pamela
Walker

George Jr
Brown

Cedric
Brown

Courtney
Hill

Amanda Casey
Hill

Grandchildren

Great-Grandchildren

Descendants of Willis Sr Hill (5 of 5)

Nathaniel Hill 1915 - ═ Mildred Harris 1918 -

Grandchildren

Great-Grandchildren

2nd Great-Grandchildren

Cont. p. 2

Allen Hafford 1939 -

Delores Hill 1939 -

Mickey Cunningham

Carolyn Hill 1942 -

Lloyd May 1945 -

Earlene Hill 1943 -

David Jones

Freddie Lee Hill 1946 - 1993

Antoinette Harper

Ronnie Hill 1951 -

Juanita Lige 1951 -

Gloria Jean Hill 1956 -

John R Dobbs

Shawn Hafford 1973 -

John R Jr Dobbs

Tonya Dobbs

Cassetta Hill

Feliz Hill 1973 -

Dennis Simth 1971 -

LaTeesha Hill 1977 -

Ronnie Jr Hill 1987 -

Lisa Hafford 1958 -

Thomas Phillips 1957 -

Mickey Cunningham

Kimberly Hafford 1962 -

Anthony Rice 1952 -

Allen Jr Hafford 1967 -

Jazmin Dennise Simth 1997 -

Jialen LaSean Simth 2001 -

Li Dairious Phillips 1979 -

La Detres Phillips 1980 -

Landry Phillips 1988 -

Towanna Rice 1982 -

Shavanna Rice 1986 -

Anthony Jr Rice 1987 -

Part One: Recollections of My Parents and Family

1927 – 1951

James (Jack) Walker   Carrie Mason Walker
(Paternal Grandparents)

**General George Washington
Monroe Gaines Hill
(Granddaddy Wash)
&
Solonie Hill**

(Maternal Grandparents)

Chapter 1

1927: LOVE at FIRST SIGHT

Granddaddy Jim, my paternal grandfather, was on his way home from work in the fields in rural Colquitt County, Georgia. He stopped to talk with his sister–in-law, Faustine Hall. Grandmama Carrie and the children were at home. Suddenly, a big storm came up. Grandmama Carrie tersely commanded Daddy, Uncle J. T., and Maggie, "Hurry! Get under the bed!" Granddaddy Jim and Aunt Faustine had started running toward the house. Without warning, the wind started lifting the house off the ground.

"Jump! Jump out the window!" they yelled to Grandmama Carrie and the children. Daddy jumped. But Uncle J. hesitated. There was a loud noise, and then the house broke apart! Both of them landed on the ground. Grandmama sustained a broken arm; Uncle J. broke his back. Daddy sustained a deep gash cut in his shoulder. No one received medical care. Grandmama put a splint on her arm and took care of Uncle J and herself as best she could. However, Uncle J was left with a weak back all his life.

"Soon after that, Papa left home, and didn't come back," was Daddy's sad commentary on the breakup of his family. Daddy was in the eighth grade at the time He had to quit school and help take care of the family; in fact, he assumed duties as head of the household. While in school, he excelled in mathematics, his favorite subject. He had been the quarterback for the football team. He liked that as well. At age 14, he stood about 5' 8" tall, and had a stocky build. His color was dark brown, and his smile revealed a set of white, straight teeth. He had an affable manner and exuded self-confidence. I never heard him express anger at being forced to leave school; he just made the most of the education he earned.

Daddy had also fallen in love with a young girl named Pauline Hill. Very attractive, she had light brown complexion, long black hair, and high cheekbones like her biological mother. Grandmama Virginia was part Cherokee.

Mama had grayish-green eyes like her daddy, Granddaddy Hill was born to a light skinned Negro mother and her white owner. He was

3

given an impressive name: General George Washington Monroe Gaines Hill. He was called Washington Hill. He would tell tales of how the children in the house were fed: Their breakfast was buttermilk with cornbread crumbled in it, and it was placed in a trough in the kitchen of the big house. The children lined up to eat like pigs feeding from a trough.

According to Aunt Teddy, Mama was the favorite child of my grandparents. She was slender and shy in mannerisms. When she smiled she revealed a separation between her front teeth. When she met Daddy, she was 5'5" tall. She never grew any taller, but Daddy continued to grow until he reached 5'9 1/2".

Mama was one of thirteen children in a blended family. When Granddaddy Hill married for the first time, his wife, Elizabeth died and left him with two daughters, Aunt Gussie, and Aunt Elizabeth. During his second marriage, he and Grandmama Virginia had five children: Aunt Thelma (Teddy), Uncle Washington, Uncle Walter, and, Pauline my mother. Grant George died at birth. Grandmama Virginia's death left Granddaddy with four more children.

Then Granddaddy met and married Grandmama Solonie Hill. She had three sons from a previous marriage to Willis Hill, Sr.: Uncle Willis, Uncle Joseph, and Uncle Nathaniel. Grandmama Solonie was the only Grandmama I remember. She was twenty years younger than Granddaddy Hill. Together, they had four more children: Aunt Solonie Bell, Uncle Lauray, Aunt Odessa, and Aunt Jessie. Mama and Aunt Teddy did not remember their stepmother favorably. I suspect that is one reason they were eager to leave home so young.

After Daddy quit school, he continued to call on my mother at her home.

Daddy's maturity and hard work ethic impressed my maternal grandparents. They approved of his courting my mother, who had fallen in love with him. When she became pregnant, she too quit school. She and my daddy married February 15, 1930 at the courthouse in Colquitt County. She was fifteen years old and he was sixteen. I was born September 21, 1930.

4

Chapter 2

1930: A ROUGH START for TEENAGERS

Mrs. Eva Alston was the black community midwife. She assisted Mama with my delivery. She came regularly to our home nearly every two years as more children were born. On May 28, 1932, she helped deliver Pearline. Two years after that, she returned to help deliver Betty Dean on May 25, 1934. Mama's fourth pregnancy resulted in the birth of my first brother, Anderson, Jr. By the time Daddy was 23 and Mama 22 they were the parents of four children.

The Walker siblings arrived in two sets: Odessa Ree, Pearline, Betty Dean, and Anderson, Jr. comprise the first set. After a five year hiatus, set two were born: Freddie James, September 8, 1941; Oreatha Laverne, April 20, 1943; Andrea Christine, August 14, 1945; and Kenneth O'Neal, September 25, 1946. Woodrow Jerome, the ninth child arrived five years later, April 21, 1951. He was the only baby Mama delivered in the hospital. He was born during my senior year in college.

Mama and Daddy began their married lives as sharecroppers on a farm in Norman Park, Georgia since they had no marketable skills and had not finished high school. Although they had no money, Daddy was determined to take care of his family, and he was equally determined that Mama would stay at home to raise the children.

My maternal grandparents lived in a big house on a farm, which they did not own. They worked the farm for a white landlord. Mama and Daddy were offered a shack across the field behind Granddaddy Hill. Daddy told of his recollections of that time:

"Your mama and I had worked hard to put in a crop of tobacco. It was growing fine, and things began to look promising. But a hailstorm destroyed the crop! I was so worried: how was I going to pay the rent? I tried to figure out what to do. Some of your uncles and other field hands told me to move during the night. That way, the landlord wouldn't know where to find us. But that didn't sound right to me, so I went to see Rev. Crouch. He told me to pray. I did. The next day, the

5

white owner came to your mama and me and said, 'Anderson, you and Pauline can work in my tobacco field; I'll pay you good.'"

They worked, earned enough to make ends meet, and Daddy said he learned his first lesson in depending on God. In 1932, he hired Grandmama Carrie, Aunt Maggie, and Uncle J. to help in the fields while he went into town to work as a butcher at Swift Meatpacking Plant.

Daddy didn't have a car. Because he had to walk to work, he would get up at three o'clock each morning for the seven-mile hike to the factory. Mama got up with him and fed him a good breakfast because he wouldn't get another hot meal until he returned home for dinner. There were no paved highways in the country. Daddy walked through the fields and took short cuts en route to work each day. If he arrived too early for work, he would lie down in a ditch and rest. Daddy never mentioned whether he met mean dogs or mean people during the 2 1/2-hour walk. After an eight-hour day, he would walk home again. Mama served dinner when Daddy returned home.

I always wondered what my daddy did at the meatpacking plant. Years later, when I was in the sixth grade, our teacher took us on a field trip to Swift's Meatpacking Plant. For the first time I saw my daddy at work. He was dressed in rubber coveralls and knee high rain boots. He had a steel mesh glove on his left hand. He worked with his right hand (the steel glove prevented cuts to his left hand).

The scene represented the most gruesome thing I had ever witnessed! As the cows came up a ramp, they were suddenly hit in the head; their hind legs were simultaneously snatched from under them. As they squealed in this suspended position, the men on the line took turns performing different tasks. Daddy would grab the bloody squealing cow and begin to separate it from its skin. His hands moved so swiftly! I stood and watched in horror. Another butcher would cut the entrails out. I was spellbound! As the class moved on, I began to walk backward, my eyes glued on my dad, yet trying to follow the class.

Suddenly, Daddy's face froze, and yelled at me, "Dessa Ree, look where you're going!" I stopped in my tracks and looked around. I was near some metal stairs. If I had fallen down those stairs, I would have

6

been seriously injured – or killed! I gathered myself and proceeded to follow the class. Perhaps that experience influenced my dislike of beef. To this day, it is one of my least favorite foods. After work, Daddy cleaned up, re-dressed in his own clothes, and walked home.

One of Daddy's goals was to save money to buy a used car. It was a T Model Ford, I think. I remember it had to be hand cranked and allowed to warm up before he drove off. Another goal was to save enough to buy a house.

As a four-year-old, my recollection of our rented house in the country was that it was a shack. There were two rooms: one large room, which was our bedroom, and a kitchen. There was a fireplace in the large room, two beds, and a window. There was no insulation; in fact, Mama stuffed the pine knotholes with rags to keep the wind out. When we stood in front of the fireplace to get warm, we would burn our legs but our backs remained cold.

There was a woodburning stove in the kitchen, a table, and two benches, one on each side of the table. In the backyard, Mama had a big, black pot where she boiled clothes. Immediately outside the kitchen door, to the right was a bench on which sat three tin tubs: one was for washing clothes, the other two for rinsing them. The immediate area around the house was free of weeds and brush. Every Monday was wash day. After the clothes were hung on the clotheslines, the water from the wash pot was used to scrub the bare wood floors. The house was located away from the main road and accessed by a path that ran from my maternal grandparents' house on the main road.

There was not a lot of housekeeping to do. Most of the time was spent in preparing meals, washing, and ironing clothes, and keeping the grounds cleared to discourage visits from animals.

Grandmama Hill's big garden supplied fresh vegetables every day. One of my fondest memories was burying sweet potatoes and covering them with pine needles. Later in the year, we would cook them in ashes in the fireplace.

When Granddaddy and some other farmers killed a hog, we smoked the meat in the smokehouse. Immediately after the hogs were killed, we had pork chops and chitterlings. There was enough meat to last for the year: ham, bacon, hog jowls, pickled pig's feet, lard, pork skins, pig ears, and souse meat. Good use was made of all the hog. Grandmama would make cracklin' bread with some of the pork skins. Food was plentiful for most of the year.

Grandmama, Mama, and some farm wives had quilting bees. They would stretch the patched fabric between two sawhorses and sit around and sew while talking. The children ran around and played.

When we harvested sugar cane, it was syrup-making time. Festivities always accompanied this activity. While the men ran the cane stalks through the wringers, which were powered by the mules that walked around in circles, the children played around the fire. We drank the cold juice. I remember it was very sweet and very filling; I could never drink a whole cup. Elders boiled the juice in a big pot until it thickened to syrup consistency. As it cooked, foam was skimmed off the top. The women helped put the dark, thick molasses in jars or jugs. It tasted especially good in the winter months with biscuits and bacon and eggs and cold milk. Grandmama and Granddaddy had cows, hogs, and chickens. The cows and chickens gave us plenty of milk and eggs. We even ate chickens occasionally. There was more milk than we could drink; some of it was set on the hearth and allowed to curdle. Then the buttermilk was churned. This caused the butter to come to the surface. It was skimmed from the top of the milk and rinsed off. Now there was butter and fresh buttermilk.

Life was very secure for the children. Our chores included picking fresh vegetables every day, shelling peas and beans, and gathering fruits for canning. There was enough work to keep us gainfully engaged, especially during harvesting. There was little time left for idleness and bickering.

Of course there were also some unpleasant memories. I remember that Granddaddy Hill had several greyhound hunting dogs. Sometimes their target was not wild game. I remember one day the baying of the hounds attracted me; they were on the path of a catch. I was shocked when I saw what they were chasing; it was a yellow cat named "Tom". The cat ran as fast as he could and scurried up a tree. These long dogs were jumping off the ground trying to reach the cat. They eventually dislodged him from the tree. I watched in horror as

8

they attacked the cat as he fell to the ground. They ripped him to pieces! The shocked reaction affected me deeply. From that time on I have never liked cats. I thought of them as weak animals that did not deserve defending. But I still like dogs.

Chapter 3

1934 – 1935: A FAITHFUL FRIEND

Living in the country meant coming in contact with snakes and other animals. To help protect me from snakes and other wild animals, Daddy had trained a bulldog named "Mac." My dog Mac, was a constant and loyal companion who went with me whenever I left the house. He allowed no one to touch me, including my mother. A rule for walking in the woods was to always carry a stick. Daddy said a stick was useful to beat the bushes because snakes often rested under blackberry bushes.

During planting and harvesting time, one of my chores was to take water to the field for Daddy and Granddaddy. One day, when I was sent to take water to the field, Mac ran ahead of me. I was aimlessly walking along the path, which followed a stream when I heard Mac growling and saw him shaking something. He had come upon a rattlesnake and proceeded to kill it. When I reached Daddy, I told him what had happened. There were big tree stumps in the field, and the men suspected a rattlesnake nest was there. That evening, after work, Daddy and some of my uncles used dynamite to blast those stumps out of the ground. Several rattlesnakes were killed. Uncle Lauray brought one of the long, dead snakes to the house to scare the children. Granddaddy made him throw it away. Mac had saved me.

One day, my mother whipped me for something I had done. I don't recall what I had done to deserve a whipping; in fact, I could never understand why I received whippings. But I did get them occasionally. She closed the doors because she knew Mac would enter the house to protect me. She neglected to close the windows. Mac dashed through the window and grabbed the switch, took it out of her hand, and growled at her. She left me alone. When Daddy came home, she said to him, "Anderson, I'm going to kill that dog. Today, he started to attack me when I tried to whip Odessa." Daddy chuckled, "Pauline, you know Mac won't let anybody touch Dessa Ree. Just remember that."

I loved that ugly dog. He was my most loyal friend. He would charge anyone whom he considered a threat to me. There was an old black man who lived in a shack way back in the woods. Every afternoon, he came across the fields with a knapsack over his shoulder. Whenever he came near our house, Mac would bark at him. One day, we noticed Mac acting strangely and foaming at the mouth as he ran around in circles. He soon fell down and didn't get up. He had been poisoned. I believed that old man poisoned my dog. I grieved his death for a long time. Daddy tried to console me, but the pain was severe.

Chapter 4

1935: DIAMOND BREAD and GRASSHOPPER GREENS

When there was time to play, my sister and I played "house". We did not have toys to play with, so we made our own. There were corncob dolls, and jump ropes made from discarded clothesline. We used whatever we found. I have a scar that reminds me of how dangerous child's play can be.

One day our youngest sister Betty needed to take a nap. Mama sent Pearline and me out to play, so we wouldn't wake Betty. That day, we decided to cook dinner just like Mama was doing. For cookware, we found some jar lids; then we decided to cook greens and cornbread. We pulled grass for greens. There were plenty of grasshoppers, so we caught a couple and pulled off their heads and legs and added them to the greens. While the greens were cooking, my sister found some broken glass. I had a great idea: "Let's make diamond bread!" We agreed to mix the broken pieces of glass with dirt and call it diamonds bread. How clever we were! We mixed the bread and patted it into the jar lids.

Soon it was time to eat. We were too young to realize the danger of putting some things in our mouths, but we both knew we didn't want to eat the grasshopper greens. I decided I would eat the bread, and my sister could eat the greens. She would have no part of that idea. "No! I want the bread!" I could run faster, so I picked up the bread and started to run. She ran after me shouting, "I want the bread!" I looked back to see how close she was. At that moment, she threw a piece of glass and hit me over the corner of my right eye. The blood scared us both, so we ran home crying.

When Mama heard our distressful duet, she came out the back door. "What happened to you, Odessa?" she inquired about the bleeding. Pearline and I began talking at the same time. "Pearline hit me with a piece of glass," I began to explain. "No, Mama. Odessa took the diamond bread, and she wanted me to eat the grasshopper greens, but I wanted the bread."

My mother washed the blood off my face and found some cobwebs to put on the cut. That stopped the bleeding. We explained what had happened. The noise woke the baby. Mama seldom took sides in arguments; usually all participants were punished. So we both had to take a nap; the excitement had made us tired. That scar made by the cut from the glass saved my life. If I had eaten that bread—and I had planned to eat it—the glass would have cut my stomach. I would probably have died from internal bleeding. I marvel at God's grace!

Chapter 5

1935: SNAKES, COUSIN, and FIRECRACKERS

Our cousin, Allen, lived in town. One day, when he was visiting, Mama and Daddy needed to harvest the sugar cane. Betty was asleep, so Mama left Pearline, Allen, and me saying, "You all can bring the baby to the field when she wakes up."

When the baby awoke, we went to the field to join Mama and Daddy. Allen was one year older than I was – and stronger, so he carried Betty because she was still a toddler. But, because we were of little help, Mama kept the baby and sent Pearline, Allen, and me back home. On the way back to the house, we encountered a black snake. Too innocent to realize the danger, we began poking at the snake with sticks. Instead of running from us, the snake moved toward us. We all ran in different directions. I arrived home first and ran into the back door. Then I sprinted back out the back door and went around the house to see where Pearline and Allen were. The snake was crawling on the front door! We decided not to tell Mama and Daddy what had happened.

Giving birth to three children in four years was hard on Mama. Daddy tried to relieve her by dropping me off at Grandmama's house on his way to work in the morning. On his way home in the evening, he picked me up. Four of my aunts and uncles were still living at home. Aunt Solonie Bell, Uncle Lauray, and Aunt Odessa were not much older than I was; Jessie Pearl was younger. Aunt Bell and Lauray were my playmates at Grandmama's house. They must have resented my presence because they teased me all the time. They called me "Goo Goo Eyes" and "Crybaby." Then they would run and hide from me. Often this teasing reduced me to tears.

After a while, I would go inside the house to be with Grandmama who seemed always to be in the kitchen. I would get the broom and voluntarily sweep the floor. Grandmama praised me for "being smart." Then she would call Aunt Bell and Lauray and tell them to go and pick blackberries so she could make a pie for that "smart gal." At dinner, my tormentors were not allowed to eat any pie until I took the first piece. This action angered my aunt and uncle, so the next day the

14

teasing started all over again. Sometimes, Grandmama asked Granddaddy to give them a whipping. Of course, I was blamed for that as well.

My dad was very protective of me. When he learned what was happening, he tried to comfort me. One day, he brought home a dark green book with a picture of a girl running with a dog on the cover. Every evening, he would read the story to me. Then one day he said, "Tomorrow, Sister, you will read the story to me."

Of course, I wanted to please my dad, so I looked at the words as he read and pointed to the words. I memorized the stories and somehow I began to associate the words with what I remembered. Within two weeks, I began reading; so, instead of going to Grandmama's house, I would stay home and help Mama with my younger sisters. In between chores, I read my book.

Another thing Daddy did was to buy me a bicycle and teach me how to ride it. I recall how patiently he held the seat while I learned to pedal. On my first solo try around the house, I ran into Mama's wash tubs and dislodged them from the bench. The tubs crashed down with a loud noise, and I fell and skinned my knee. After Mama restored order, I tried again. Very soon, I had two engaging activities: reading my book and riding my bike.

Other pleasant memories come to mind. One that still brings warm feelings to me is the effort my parents put into making Christmas a happy time for us. Daddy worked for the Swift Meatpacking Plant; they gave bonuses to their employees – on Christmas Eve. When I was five years old, Daddy came home early and he and Mama went shopping for as many gifts as they could buy with his bonus. One of the outstanding gifts that Christmas was a red wagon. We all took turns riding in and pulling the wagon. Each year we looked forward to waking up to the surprises: oranges, tangerines, peppermint stick candy, various kinds of nuts, including coconuts, and fireworks. With his pocketknife, Daddy would cut a hole in top of our oranges and we would put the peppermint stick in the hole and suck the juice of the orange through the peppermint. He would crack the coconut and pour out the coconut milk for us to drink. Mama used the coconut meat to make ambrosia. In fact, the only time Mama made cakes was at Christmas and Easter. They were cooked on top of the stove in a wrought iron pancake pan. She made thin layers, then stacked them with apple jelly between the layers. They were delicious! There were probably many happy children at Christmas time in our town, but none were happier than the Walker children were. Daddy showed us how to light Roman candles and the sparklers. We squealed our delight at the sparkles. Our cousin, Allen got firecrackers for Christmas. He boastingly showed how he could light them and throw them before they exploded.

Chapter 6

1935 – 1936: SIBLING RIVALRY

I recall one especially memorable Christmas when I was about seven years old. We had moved to a bigger house, and Daddy hired one of the men from a neighboring farm to play Santa Claus for us. The men in that family were very good carpenters, so Daddy hired them to make for us a child sized doll house, complete with small furniture! My two sisters and I loved playing in that house that Santa Claus brought. By now, our brother, Anderson, Jr. the fourth child was nearly two years old, just old enough to be a bother. He insisted on playing with us, and Mama agreed that he should. "He's your little brother and you should play with him," she'd say.

But he was so destructive! For some reason, he decided to sit on the doll dresser! His weight crushed it! We cried and told Mama what he had done. "Anderson, Jr., why did you break the dresser?" "Mama, I just sat down on it, and it broke." "He didn't mean to do it," she said to us. To Junior she said, "Be careful; don't break your sisters' things." Our solution was to go and play at something else that excluded him, so we jumped rope. His response was to throw rocks at us. Even so, Christmas was almost always a happy time for us.

The inclusion of our brother brought unwelcome changes in our ordered lives. The next Christmas, my grandmama bought me a big doll; the doll seemed to be as big as I was. Anderson, Jr. was forbidden to play with it. One day as we were standing on the porch watching the rain (we were not allowed to play in the rain), I was hugging my doll. Quicker than a flash, Anderson, Jr. yanked my doll from my arms and threw it out into the rain. I still remember the sinking feeling as I watched helplessly as the rain peeled the skin from my doll. I was heartbroken.

Chapter 7

1936: STARTING SCHOOL

Education was very important to Daddy and Mama. He had taught me to read in anticipation of my starting school. One day when I was old enough to start school, Daddy came home and announced, "Next week Dessa Ree will start school. I asked Miz Mederine to come by and pick her up and take her to school." Mrs. Mederine Wise was the teacher at the one room schoolhouse. She had a car, and she agreed to pick me up and take me to school if the weather allowed.

The first day soon arrived. Mama woke me up early and combed and braided my hair. After breakfast I put on a fresh starched dress. I had no idea what school would be like, but I trusted my dad completely. If he said this was what I needed, then I must make the best of it.

The school was a white clapboard building with a signboard for announcements in the front. It was the same building we worshipped in each Sunday. When I stepped inside, I saw about thirty black children, ranging in grades from one to seven. The first graders sat on the first pew, the second graders sat on the third pew; third graders sat on the fifth pew. At the front of the room was a large potbellied stove. A small table on the left side of the room served as Miz Mederine's desk.

After opening with a song, prayer, and pledge to the flag, the school day began. Miz Mederine met first with the first graders. After she gave us our assignment, she reminded us to work quietly with our slates and books and not disturb the other children. There was a long switch in the corner in plain view to remind us what would happen if we disobeyed. It was easy for me to keep quiet because I wanted to listen to the assignments given to the others. Learning was so exciting! My dad and I discussed what I had learned each day. He had taught me how to read, so school excited me.

At the end of the year my teacher gave the students a test to determine whether we passed to the next grade. I successfully tested out at the fourth grade level! My dad was so proud; I was happy to make my dad proud of me.

18

"Just think of what you could have done if you could have gone to school every day!" he said. Because school was too far for me to walk, we depended on Mrs. Wise to pick me up. She was happy to do so when the road was passable. If it rained too hard, the unpaved road was muddy and her car might get stuck in the mud. I went to school whenever the weather permitted.

Chapter 8

1937 – 1938: MOVE to TOWN

Before school started the next year, we moved to town. Daddy had saved enough money to have a house built for us. It was small—three rooms and a kitchen, and a front and back porch. It was new! And it was ours! There were electric lights, but no indoor plumbing. Daddy planned to add that later. I remember how wide our eyes opened when my cousin switched the lights on. He pushed a switch on the wall and the light came on in the ceiling. It was magic! We made a game of switching the lights off and on until Daddy said to stop.

Our new house was sparsely furnished at first. However, we brought along beds and some valuable items from the farm. I remember the back porch was piled high with sugar cane. At nights after work, Daddy would sometimes peel cane for us. It was so sweet.

High weeds and brush surrounded our new house. Granddaddy gave Mama a cow named Bossy. She roamed the field between the house and the outhouse. Bossy supplied plenty of milk for our family. Under Mama's tutelage, I learned to milk her. Sometimes, I would squirt the milk directly into my mouth. It was warm and sweet. I don't remember exactly how long we had Bossy; I don't think it was for a long time because there was no place to house her. There were no other houses near ours: just lots of bushes and weeds. In my mind, snakes lived in the brush. The toilet was an outhouse; I dreaded going out there. In addition to spiders, lizards and other creepy crawlers, occasionally we would see a snake. So I decided I would rather use the high grass near the house and near Bossy. Mama saw me do this and she said I should go to the outhouse. However, when I thought she was not looking, I still used the field. One day, she said to me, "I know you think I don't see you, but remember, even if I don't see you, God does." After that, when I had to use the bathroom, I would look around to see if God was looking, and if I didn't see Him, I used the field!

Daddy soon rescued us; he had a toilet built on the back porch. Saturday nights, we bathed in a tin tub behind the stove. There was a big wood burning stove in the kitchen; a water tank was attached.

20

Mama heated water in the tank while she cooked, and we heated more water on the stove in large pots. Each of us took turns bathing in the tub. Mama hung a sheet to give us privacy.

Chapter 9

1938: TRANSFERRING SCHOOLS, REPEATING GRADES

During the summer 1938, it was time to register for school in the new Moultrie, Georgia school district. My sister, Pearline was now old enough to attend school. Daddy took my sister Pearline and me to register. He showed the school administrators my report card, which indicated that I was ready to begin fourth grade. Coming from the country, the school staff ignored my grades. My sister and I were placed together in low first (today called kindergarten). Two weeks later, Mrs. Larrimore called me to her desk and said, "Little Girl, you don't belong with me; I'm sending you to high first with Mrs. Baker."

Because I had not yet made any friends, at recess I played with my sister and her friends. In class, a boy named Ralph McBride sat behind me and pinched my neck. It hurt, but I didn't cry out or tell the teacher. My dad noticed the bruises on my neck and asked me what had happened. I told him this boy named Ralph McBride pinched my neck. Daddy said, "The next time he pinches you, you turn around and hit him as hard as you can. When you get out of school, haul pork – run!"

The next day, after recess, while Mrs. Baker was reading the class a story about a grasshopper, Ralph pinched me. I turned around and hit him as hard as I could and he fell out of his chair. The commotion caused Mrs. Baker to look up. She noticed that I was turned in my seat and Ralph was on the floor. She asked me, "What is the story about?" I replied, "A hoppergrass."

She sent me to the cloakroom, and she came in and paddled me with a ruler. I was more shocked and humiliated than hurt, but I don't remember anything else that happened that day. At home that evening at dinner I told Daddy what happened. He got in his car immediately and went to see Mrs. Baker. The next morning in class, Mrs. Baker called Ralph and me to her desk. She looked at my neck and showed it to Ralph. "How did this happen?" He confessed he had done it. So, Mrs. Baker took Ralph to the cloakroom! He never pinched me again. At recess, I still played with my sister and her friends.

22

Just before the Christmas holiday, Mrs. Baker called me to her desk and told me that I should report to Mrs. Hall when we returned to school. Mrs. Hall was the second grade teacher. I remained in second grade for two weeks; then, I was sent to Mrs. Watts, the third grade teacher's class.

One day, during recess just before I returned to class, I needed to use the bathroom. This made me late to class. Mrs. Watts sent me to the cloakroom and swatted me. I was angry and humiliated; in fact, I left school and went home. Mama was sitting in the front porch swing. I told her what had happened. To my relief, she didn't send me back to school. When Daddy came home, I told him what happened. He went to see Mrs. Watts. The next day she asked me why I hadn't told her I was late because I was in the bathroom when the bell rang. I said, "You didn't ask me why I was late; you just whipped me." She never did again, but she was always cool toward me. I never learned to like Mrs. Watts.

At the end of the year, I was promoted to the fourth grade! When school started the following year, I made friends with a girl named Willie Louis. We always played and stayed together. One day, as we were lining up to return to class after recess, an older classmate named Teresa, got in line in front of Willie Louis. When Willie objected, Teresa shoved Willie, and Willie began to cry. I came to her defense, and began arguing with Teresa. Mrs. Washington said nothing until we returned to class. Teresa and I were still arguing. Mrs. Washington told us to go to the front of the class. She gave us boxing gloves and challenged us to settle the argument. I didn't know how to fight. One of the boys was putting coal into the potbellied stove. I rammed my head into Teresa's stomach and pushed her toward the open stove door. Burned, she cried out! The class started egging me on. Mrs. Washington stopped the fight and restored order quickly. That was my first and last fight at school. For some unknown reason, no one ever challenged me again.

Chapter 10

1939 – 1940: SERIOUS ACCIDENT with FIRE

But the fourth grade year stands out in my mind for other reasons. I was nine years old. One day, after I returned home from school, Mama told me to make a fire in the stove so she could cook dinner. I laid the wood and looked for the kerosene to help start the fire. Mama was sitting on the front porch in the swing. I asked her the location of the kerosene. She told me to look for a quart jar near the storage house. The jar I selected was a quart jar in which my dad had a car part soaking in gasoline. Not knowing the difference, I poured some of it on the wood in the stove. I struck the match, poked my head in to get a good view of where to light the fire. Whoosh! Startled and scared because the fire had ignited my clothes, I ran out the back door and around the house. Mama was sitting in the swing on the front porch. She tackled me and rolled me on the ground. She doused the flames, but I was badly burned. Mama stripped off my clothes, covered my hands and face with Vaseline, and put me to bed.

When I awoke, Daddy was home. He took me to see the white Dr. Joiner. To my knowledge, this was the first time I had ever been taken to see a doctor. Dr. Joiner worked deftly as Daddy recounted to him what had happened. The doctor stripped the burned skin from the first and second fingers of the right hand. Then he applied ointment to my hand and wrapped it in layers of bandages. He also gave Daddy medicine to apply to my face. My eyelids and lashes were singed off. It was necessary for Daddy to take me back to have the dressings changed as Dr. Joiner monitored the healing.

After a few weeks, I returned to school, but could not write for the remainder of the year. Mrs. Washington administered my tests orally. I had also missed the introduction to long division. When Mrs. Washington sent me to the chalkboard, I felt so humiliated! My response was to burst into tears. "Don't cry, Honey. I'll help you. You can stay in at recess time and I'll help you." This suited me fine. I did not want to try to answer all the questions my classmates kept asking about my bandages.

24

As my hand healed, I developed sores in my scalp. My hair had to be shaved off my head around the sores. And I developed athlete's foot. I was reduced to wearing a white sock on my foot until I could again wear a shoe. I fell into a depression for school was no longer fun for me. I had lost so much schoolwork due to absences, and I could not easily catch up. One night, I heard my parents discussing me in their bedroom. Mama began to cry. I suspect she felt some guilt for what happened to me. They found what they considered a solution to lift my spirits. Mama wrote to her sister in Cincinnati, and Aunt Teddy made me three new dresses. They were beautiful! And, I was sent to Aunt Faustine to have my hair done. These acts of kindness lifted my spirits. I felt very special when classmates commented about my new dresses and my pressed and curled hair.

Chapter 11

1940: DADDY DECIDES I MUST PLAY the PIANO

The crowning distraction was to have me take piano lessons. Daddy wanted all of us to take music lessons, but could pay for only one; so, being the oldest, I was chosen. He took me to Mrs. Singquefield's house, and told her he wanted me to learn to play the piano. I knew nothing about a piano, but if my Daddy wanted me to learn to play it, I would try. Again, learning something new fascinated me. Daddy could not pay for piano lessons and buy a piano at the same time, so I practiced on a cardboard keyboard at the kitchen table. I went to lessons once per week. Each time I returned home, I had to teach my sister, Pearline, what Mrs. Singquefield had taught me. That meant paying close attention to what she said. Mama's contribution was to visit the table frequently and ask, "Are you sure you're using the right fingers?"

I only heard the music when I played it at the teacher's house. I taught Pearline and Pearline taught Betty. Betty tried to teach Junior; he simply would not cooperate! Daddy got three lessons for the price of one! Mama said he's smart, and he was.

Within a year, Daddy bought a piano, a magnificent instrument! It was a player piano; all of us could play it. And we did! We enjoyed watching the notes go up and down as we pedaled and the tape played. This continued for a while; eventually, Daddy thought we needed to really concentrate on playing it ourselves, so he removed the player portion.

Later, Daddy was able to afford for Pearline and Betty to take lessons. Of the nine children, six learned to play a musical instrument. Pearline, Betty, Oreatha, Andrea, and I learned to play the piano. My brother, Freddie learned to play the coronet and Woodrow played the trumpet.

Our dad was remarkable! Many Saturday nights, we would all join in the family sing time. Daddy played the guitar, I played the piano, and we all sang. Daddy would even bring home bananas or cookies as treats. Those were enjoyable times.

On Sundays, Daddy accompanied us to Sunday school and church. Mama almost always stayed home with the baby. I learned later that she felt she never had proper clothes to wear to church. After her childbearing years, however, she became very active in the church, singing in the choir and joining with women's groups.

Because of excessive absences during fourth grade, I really fell far behind, especially in reading. I began to avoid reading. My teacher spoke to Daddy and speculated that I might have sustained damage to my eyes when I was burned. A trip to the eye doctor confirmed that I needed glasses. Instead of being ashamed to wear them, I was happy that I could now see clearly. I worked hard to regain my academic proficiency, and over time I began to again excel in school. I did not welcome summer vacation; I wanted to go to school year round.

While in elementary school, two more accidents happened that interrupted my regained confidence. During the summer following fifth grade, while riding home on my bicycle, I took a short cut through an alley. There was a slight hill, so I got off the bike and started to push it. Without warning, a dog lurched from under a house and sank her teeth into my left leg. I ran home screaming. Daddy was at home and took me immediately to see Dr. Samuel, the only African American doctor in Moultrie. Daddy had often taken Dr. and Mrs. Samuel on trips to visit places out of town; neither of them could drive. What Dr. Samuel did to my leg hurt more than the bite. He cauterized it. There was no way of knowing if the dog had rabies and no way of finding out, I guess. He used something that looked like an over sized Q-Tip. He dipped the cotton-covered end into a black solution and pushed it into the wound made by the dogbite. Daddy had to hold me down as I screamed and squirmed. It was necessary to revisit Dr. Samuel two or three times. Fortunately, the wound didn't swell or become infected. It healed, although the scar remains.

One day later that spring I was involved in an automobile accident, while Daddy was driving me to my music lesson. At an intersection, a driver ignored the stop sign and struck us on the passenger side of the car. I was thrown through the windshield. There were no seatbelts at that time. I did not lose consciousness; I heard Daddy say to someone who was looking at the accident, "Take us to the hospital!"

African Americans were not treated at the hospital except in emergencies. Dr. Joiner came to the hospital. I wasn't hurt badly: A few scratches and bruises, and the breath was knocked out of me. I marvel at God's grace and care and a dad's courage and wisdom!

Mama always waited for Daddy to come home before she served dinner. When we were served meat, Daddy always cleaned the meat off the bones after we finished, saying, "You all don't know what's good; you leave the best part on the bones." I wondered why Daddy liked the bones better than the meat. I later realized that he wanted to be sure we had enough to eat first; then he would eat what was left over. At dinner we also brought Daddy up- to- date on all the happenings at school, and asked for all the things that we wanted him to buy for us! Poor Daddy. He didn't seem to mind. He would tell us if we could afford it, or if we couldn't. More often we couldn't. Yet, Daddy would chuckle as he said, "I'm one of the richest men in town. All my children are healthy and full of wants!"

Chapter 12

1942 – 1943: DEVELOPING a THICK SKIN

As I came into the sixth grade I became more observant of my surroundings. Moultrie High School for Negro Youth was the school for colored children in Moultrie, GA. There was a large campus; in the center of the campus was a flagpole. An ambitious shop teacher, Mr. Simmons, engaged the boys in shop to lay a concrete walkway all around the campus. Everyone appreciated it because the grounds had no grass, only sand. The building housing primary classes was located on the east of the campus. On the opposite side, about eighty yards across, was the elementary building. Grades three through six were housed there. The largest building on the south side was the high school. Classes started there in grade seven. And, to the north were the home economics and shop buildings.

For the first time in my school life I had a male teacher, Mr. A. F. Shaw. He was a good teacher. But he had a sharp and sometimes biting tongue. I interpreted it as trying to embarrass us.

When I started sixth grade, Mama demanded that I wash the dishes and clean the kitchen every morning before I departed for school. Pearline, Betty, and Anderson Jr. took their sweet time eating breakfast. I yelled at them to hurry up, but they seldom cooperated. Although I lived only a block from the school, and sprinted all the way, I was always late.

Mr. Shaw always said something to embarrass me. For example, he'd say, "Odessa Ree, you live just across the street. Why can't you get to school on time? You're going to be late to your own funeral!" Of course, the class laughed. I wanted to arrive at school on time. Every day I tried again to get my brother and sisters to eat quickly so I could clean the dishes and get to school on time. They didn't seem to care; mama didn't seem to care. So I decided I didn't care either.

I began to develop a thick skin. When Mr. Shaw made smart aleck remarks, I ignored him. I also ignored the class for laughing. I felt that they were all uncaring and insensitive. Having developed a thick skin and learning how to "play it cool" proved to be helpful later in life when

I became a teacher. This same attitude served me well when I encountered the big world of segregationist attitudes where I was often subjected to biting and hateful remarks from people who should have known better; especially some teachers who were mean, and some spiteful, controlling whites.

Every day, Mr. Shaw left the class after lunch to go to the office. He told us to work on an assignment. Immediately after he left, some of the students started acting up. One day Jay said to Homer, "Get Geneva!" The idiot did just that. He got out of his seat, went over to her desk, and started wrestling her. She struggled with him but she lost, and began to cry. A few of the class thought this was funny. I didn't. This same scene was played out day after day. Geneva always ended up crying. Two weeks went by; I could take it no longer. So I said to Homer," If you want to fight, why don't you pick on someone your size?" Suddenly the room was silent. I had everyone's attention. They couldn't believe that shy, quiet Odessa was challenging Homer to a fight. He was surprised as well. "You want to fight me?" "Yes!" At that moment, Mr. Shaw returned to the classroom. We resumed our lesson. The next day, when Mr. Shaw left the classroom, Jay urged Homer to fight Geneva. He turned and looked at me. "You really want to fight me?" "I will if you hit Geneva again." He believed me. He didn't hit her. Or me.

At recess, he came up to me and asked, "Why did you take up for Geneva?" "You act like a trained dog," I replied. "Jay says, 'Jump', and you jump. Can't you think for yourself?" "You know, I really didn't want to fight Geneva, but, if I didn't, the other kids would laugh at me." "And you are willing to hurt her rather than think for yourself?" "You're right. You were brave to do what you did. Thank you."

That day, I learned to stand up for what I believed. A friendship was born! Homer and I became best friends. We looked for each other on the school grounds. There was so much to talk about. He respected my independence: I liked his honesty.

I learned that he lived diagonally across the street from my piano teacher. His family owned a corner store. He began to watch for me when I came to music lessons. He would bribe his brother to cover for him while he walked me part of the way home. Soon our names were linked together as sweethearts; we were flattered, but thought of ourselves only as friends.

He was not the only one to begin to take note of me. Mrs. Westmoreland, the fifth grade teacher led an effort to choose students to participate in school talent shows. One day she came into our sixth grade classroom and asked if she could take some of the students out of class and teach them some dance steps. She selected Rebecca Harrington and me and we both learned to tap dance. We were billed as "The Blackberry Twins." I felt cool.

Chapter 13

1943 – 1947: DANCING and SINGING MY WAY

THROUGH HIGH SCHOOL

For the rest of our high school years our dance routine was in demand for many school events. I was also included in other dance groups. Costumes were required for different performances. It seems I was always asking Daddy for money to buy a new costume. I was also selected for speaking parts in school plays. My most famous role was a lead in a play called *ONLY SALLY ANN*. I won the role in auditions. My family involved themselves in helping me practice my speaking parts. Mama recruited my brothers and sisters to read other parts and help me come in on cue. On opening night, I was hoarse. At one point in the play, I was supposed to scream. So Pearline stood in for me. Right on cue, she screamed from backstage. The play was well received in the community. After the play, several people greeted me by calling me Sally Ann.

At the beginning of the school day, all students assembled around the flagpole. We pledged to the flag, listened to announcements, then concluded with calisthenics. For a while, I was chosen to lead the school in calisthenics. And, I excelled in my studies. During high school, I always ranked in the top 5% of the class.

I also became a member of the school choir. For evening performances Daddy was always present. Mama always stayed home with the younger children. I loved my Daddy for the time he devoted to us children. As I grew older, I learned to appreciate the sacrifices my mother made in rearing us as well.

Chapter 14

1944: SUMMER in CINCINNATI

When I was nearly fourteen years old, Mama sent me to Cincinnati to help my aunt Solonie Bell who was experiencing difficulty with a second pregnancy. Mama also required that my three-year old brother, Freddie James accompany me. The two of us traveled by train to Cincinnati, and I was to be responsible for him. Mama packed us a lunch, and Daddy drove us to the train station and bought us third class tickets. We were assigned seats in a car reserved for Negroes. Our car was almost empty.

The trip seemed to last forever. After we ate lunch, Freddie fell asleep. But I continued to look out the window at the view – fields, forests, cows, small towns, and big cities. I felt overwhelmed by the beauty, and homesick. When the train crossed the Ohio River, fear gripped me. The train terminal was awe-inspiring! I had never seen anything so big! There were so many people! No one met us at the terminal. When Freddie and I walked out of the front of the terminal, I caught my breath. The flowers and the fountain in front of the station were breathtaking. Mama had given me Aunt Bell's address, so we took a cab to her apartment.

My aunt's little girl, Bernice was five years old; I took care of her and my little brother. In addition to caring for the two young children, I helped with cleaning, cooking, and laundry. My aunt also needed constant attention because she remained sick throughout the pregnancy. My workload was oppressive. No one seemed to notice my significant responsibility for a thirteen-year-old. I received no pay. I didn't complain because Mama had instructed me to be helpful. My aunt's family lived in a third floor apartment with no air-conditioning. Often I felt like I couldn't breathe. At night, I crawled out onto the fire escape to get some fresh air. My ears were assaulted by the sounds of big city life: people talking, people fighting, radios blasting, cars screeching, and sirens wailing. I had never heard such sounds before.

Aunt Bell had a radio, which she played during the day. This was my first exposure to "Soap Operas." I overheard such shows as *All My Children* and *Hope Springs Eternal*. But the stories all seemed so sad that I stopped listening to them.

On Sundays, I was allowed to walk over to Grandmama Solonie's house, which seemed a long distance. It was confusing to find my way through the strange city. Grandmama lived in the housing projects; it was puzzling to distinguish her apartment from others that looked identical to hers. I was relieved when someone pointed out to me that I could distinguish her place by reading the number on the doorway. These visits provided me a break from my daily tasks at my Aunt Bell's house.

At the end of the summer, Mama visited Cincinnati; she brought my baby sister, Oreatha with her, who had just begun to toddle. She got into everything! As Mama constantly ran after her, I realized why Mama sent my brother with me: She was overwhelmed by her responsibilities with so many children!

Before the birth of my new cousin, Ulysses, the four of us took the train back home. Gleeful with anticipation, I looked forward to seeing Daddy and my brothers and sisters. When Daddy met us at the station, I ran toward him with outstretched arms. Daddy ran right past me and hugged and kissed Mama. I was crushed. But moments later, I felt his strong arms around me, as he said, "Dessa Ree, it seems you grew some more." I fell asleep that night to the peaceful sounds of crickets chirping. I heaved a sigh of relief. It was wonderful to be home!

Chapter 15

1945: PROTECTED by DAD'S LONG ARM

After I returned home from Cincinnati, I began to assert myself. I wanted to earn my own money. Although Daddy worked hard to provide our needs, I wanted to be able to contribute to my own upkeep -at least purchase some clothes and luxury items. Baby-sitting was the only work I was qualified to do. Taking care of my own siblings had provided me much experience. When I told Daddy I wanted to get a part-time job baby-sitting for white families, he explained, "Dessa Ree, I can't let you work for white folks because someone might hurt you and I would have to kill them. Then I wouldn't be around to watch you children grow up, and I want to be around to see you grow up." Years later, I learned that white men often sexually abused black nannies. I am glad I accepted his ruling.

Instead, because I could play the piano, Daddy agreed to let me play for church choirs. On the first and third Sundays, I played for Union Baptist Church; Willowgrove Baptist Church had services on second and fourth Sundays. The pay was not much - $5.00 per Sunday. Soon, my piano playing became known in the community. I was sought after to accompany a community choir, directed by my high school principal. Thus, I earned money to spend as I chose. Mama insisted that I share. Whenever I bought yard goods to make a dress for myself, I had to buy enough to make a dress for Pearline, too.

There was also a theater for colored people in our community. On Friday nights, there was a live talent show. Someone approached me about playing. Daddy was not pleased because he could not accompany me; and he really cared little for us attending such places. But I argued that he had said I could earn money by playing the piano. Anyway, it was in our colored community, so I would be safe. Daddy reluctantly granted me permission.

There were no streetlights in our community, so I had to walk alone in the dark. Fearlessly, I started for the theater. One block from our house, a white man pulled his car along side me and said, "Where're you going, girl?" (I could tell he was white by his voice). When I did not answer him, he stopped the car and slid over to the passenger side, opened the door, and started to get out of the car. Again, he

35

offered to give me a ride. He was so close to me, I could smell cigarette smoke on his breath. Fear gripped me. Out of the dark, I heard a voice: "Where you going, Dessa?" It was Miz. Juanita. I could discern a small tree branch in her hand.

When the white man heard her, he returned to the car and drove off. I was so relieved! I immediately went back home, explaining to Mama that I changed my mind about going to the theater. I never told Daddy what happened, but I stopped arguing his decisions.

However, the white men were not the only males his daughters needed to be protected from. There were also black teenage males. Daddy had a message for them as well. And this is how he delivered it. Every Wednesday, on the way to a second job at Felton's Dry Cleaners, Dad stopped by the pool hall to shoot a few games. A friend reported, "Mr. Anderson came in to shoot pool on Wednesday afternoon. As he aimed his cue stick to make a play, he paused and said, 'Any body mess with my daughters, will deal with me and my shotgun.' Then he sank the ball for accent."

Daddy was known as a man of his word. Although many fellows came to visit us on Sunday nights, when Mama walked past the living room door and cleared her throat at 10:00 p.m., they promptly said "goodnight."

When I was 14 years old, one morning Mama awakened me to start a fire in the heater. She observed spots of blood on my gown. She said in a matter of fact way, "Odessa, look in my top drawer and get one of those rags and put it on." She had anticipated the onset of my menses. She must have thought I knew what was happening because she didn't explain anything. I had no idea what was happening to me. Soon thereafter, our Home Economics teacher, Mrs. Brevard arranged a meeting of all the girls in the class, while the Principal met with the boys. These sex education meetings became a frequent part of our curriculum. Mrs. Brevard explained to us girls the meaning of monthly periods. Mrs. Dennis, the science teacher joined her. She explained the biology of conception and how girls got pregnant. Mrs. Dennis insisted that we should not get pregnant unless we were married. One by one they took each girl in our class aside. When my turn came, Mrs. Dennis asked me, "What would you do if you started petting and found yourself giving in to the boy?" I protested that I would not find myself in that position. She insisted, "If you do find yourself in that position, insist the boy use protection – a rubber." Daddy's response to the onset of my menses was to open a charge account at the drug store so we girls could go and purchase our needs every month.

In high school, my friends began to dwindle. It was due in part to Daddy's rules. We children were not allowed out of our yard after dark, and if friends visited our house, Mama sent them home just before our dinner hour.

One of my girlfriends, Mary Murphy and I decided to study hard to become the best in our class. Our plan was to learn at least one new word per day from the dictionary (of course we were relegated to talking with each other!). Another friend and I decided to learn to sew. In our home economics class, we were taught the basics, so we began to make some of our own clothes. Pearline became jealous, so I had to make a dress for her each time I made one for myself. However, according to her, mine always looked better than hers did, so my mother told her to make her own. She chose a plaid pattern to make a skirt. When she was ready to hem it, she trimmed the bottom by following a line in the pattern of the cloth. She wound up cutting it too short. She was so disgusted, she despaired of sewing; instead, she turned her attention to cooking, and over time she became an excellent cook.

One classmate, Walter Jackson, Jr. had a beautiful singing voice. Our music teacher, Mrs. Pettiford worked with him to hone his innate talents. Walter Jr. was awarded solo parts in the school choir, and often sang for special programs. In my sophomore year, we were teamed together to represent the school at a regional talent event. He sang and I played the piano. Mrs. Pettiford gave me two classical songs to memorize.

I tried to learn the music, but my ability was not as good as she thought it was. Meanwhile Walter Jr. got into a serious fight in which he used a knife to cut another boy's leg. As a consequence he was dropped from the talent event; still we remained friends. He got into more and more fights, and was almost suspended from school. One day three of our teachers called me in to talk about my friendship with Walter Jr. They discouraged my friendship with him because he had a

37

bad reputation. I thanked them politely, but told them that our friendship was just that: friendship only. His change in behavior concerned me, and I told him so. He felt the teachers were picking on him. He tried to improve his temper.

Daddy knew about Walter's troubles and said to me, "Dessa Ree, be careful how you choose your friends. If they are stronger than you, they will draw you to their bad ways, but if you are stronger, you will draw them to your good ways."

Chapter 16

1947: HIGH SCHOOL GRADUATION

At that time, the students at Moultrie High School for Negro Youths graduated at the end of eleventh grade. I graduated in 1947. Although seventy-five students entered high school five years earlier, only fifty students graduated. At age sixteen, I was one of the youngest graduates. Our class had the highest number of honor students and the largest number of students to enter college. There were thirteen honor students; fifteen members of our class went to college. The students with the highest grade point average spoke at the graduation exercises. The teachers allowed us to choose our speech topics. I spoke about the importance of recreation in a well-rounded life. I probably chose that topic because I had a good reputation as a talented dancer and acrobat. Many days I led calisthenics before school. Even today, I value physical fitness.

Daddy attended the graduation exercises. He was very proud of my standing in the class. He had the class picture, the picture of the honor students, and my diploma framed. They were the first framed items to hang on the walls at our home.

The summer following graduation was somewhat lonely. Most of my friends did not attend college. We seemed to have less and less in common. Many men joined the military. Homer joined so he could save money to go to college. My earning capacity was limited, so I bought very few new clothes. I was in a daze that summer. I recall reading a lot, and spending time alone. I continued to play the piano for church choirs; choir rehearsals were held two evenings per week. For the first time in my life, I realized that school provided structure for me. Now that high school was over, I asked Daddy if I could attend college. Daddy said that I could attend college; so that summer provided me time to reflect and dream about the next stage in my life.

Chapter 17

1947 – 1951: PAINE COLLEGE, AUGUSTA GEORGIA

I was the first member of my family to attend college; therefore, I knew little about what to anticipate. Neither of my parents could help. Daddy continued to work hard at two jobs; he also earned money by chauffeuring people in our community. He made it clear that he would provide the money for school; I was not to worry.

One thing Daddy bought me in preparation for attending college was a big wardrobe trunk. It wasn't a new one, but it served its intended purpose. It was too big to fit comfortably in our bedroom, so I packed it and left it in the back yard. It looked sturdy enough to withstand rain, so I was not concerned about my clothes getting wet. However, the rain seeped into it! My clothes began to bleed on each other. When I opened the trunk, I was devastated! Mama calmly took the clothes to a cleaner to have them dyed. One woolen dress that was a bright gold color was dyed maroon. All the newly dyed clothes were prettier than the original. These transformations were surprisingly pleasing.

I celebrated my seventeenth birthday in September as a college freshman. This was my first time on my own, away from my family. And the first time I experienced white teachers. And this was the first time I had been issued new textbooks.

During orientation, we learned the history of Paine College. In 1882, each Colored Methodist Episcopal Church in the Georgia conference appointed three of its members to a committee, which established Paine Institute, named in honor of Bishop Robert Paine. Six months after incorporation, classes began in rented quarters on Broad Street in Augusta, Georgia. In 1886 the school was moved to a 50-acre campus. All the physical facilities of the college are located within a geographical area bound by Fifteenth Street, Laney-Walker Boulevard, Beman Street, and Central Avenue. Most of the college buildings, including residence halls, classroom buildings and the library, are located in the main campus area. Directly across the street from this area are the athletic field, gymnasium, and the chapel/music building.

40

Dean Emma Gray said, "Paine has always been a distinctively Christian college. It maintains deep concern for the quest for truth, and has been resolute in blending knowledge with values and personal commitment."

Study was the order of the day for me. Learning new things still interested me. My coursework was standard for a Liberal Arts major: written and oral composition, mathematics, science, history, chemistry, fine arts, music, physical education, and school orientation. Because Paine was a Methodist school, we were also introduced to religious studies, which were mandatory. After settling into the routine of class attendance, I explored extra-curricular activities. In high school, I was not allowed to participate in extra activities because I had to help my mother with the children and the chores. At college, there was extra time to do some of the things I wanted to do: practice the piano, sing in the choir, and read.

For the first time I shared a room with someone who was not a member of my family. My first roommate and I were not compatible. She was two or three years older than I was. Men and dating interested her; they did not interest me. We tolerated each other, but had very little in common. She was also not truthful. I found this fact unsettling. And she stole my belongings. Mama and Pearline sent me a pretty new dress for Easter. My roommate went home for the Easter break. I did not. My new dress was missing when I got ready to wear it to Easter services. I was incredulous! Of course, I reported the missing dress to the dormitory mother. Neither of us could figure out what happened. Mrs. Gartrell, the dormitory mother, planned to confront my roommate when she returned to school. She never returned! What a loss! I never wore my new dress. The incident was so humiliating, I was ashamed to write home and tell my family what happened. I was relieved that my roommate didn't return to school. For the rest of the year, I lived alone and I liked that.

Of course, at Paine College, in 1947, social restrictions were tight. Freshmen were not allowed to leave the campus without a chaperone. We were taken to town to shop in small groups once or twice per month. The women's dormitory was off-limits to males except Sundays for three hours. Our housemother arranged the chairs for our visitors; one of the chairs faced front, and the other faced the opposite direction. The young men must keep their hands to themselves, young ladies, too. The housemother controlled the lights and the time. When she announced "young men, young ladies visiting time is over," the young men were expected to leave promptly - under her gaze! No smooching, no hand holding, only conversation in a moderate tone of voice.

These rules were fine for me. I didn't have a steady beau while at college. Homer and I had agreed that we should be free to date others, and we refrained from communicating for at least two years – to determine if we were really in love. I felt no desire to date any one else on a regular basis. For a few special occasions, I had an escort, but never became serious about a male while at college.

When I entered school in September, I gave little attention to the campus. By springtime, I became more observant of my surroundings. The path that stretched across the campus from the main building to the dormitory was lined with trees and shrubbery – with alternating purple and white blossoms, our school colors.

At Paine College, I experienced my first interracial conferences. These conferences were held regularly at the school; participation was mandatory. The experiences were unforgettable. The words of our school song came to life as we formed friendships with different races and cultures:

> And may the things, which thou hast sought,
>
> Our nation's woeful lack,
>
> True union of the hearts be brought
>
> And differences be set at naught
>
> Between the white and black.
>
> Paine College, guardian of the way
>
> That each young foot must tread,
>
> Thy gates are open to this day
>
> And our firm, martial strides display
>
> Hearts clean and unafraid.

Vv. 2,3 Paine Hymn by Frank Yerby, class of 1937; music by Mark Fax

Toward the end of the freshman year faculty urged us to declare a major. Counselors assisted us in making choices. I liked reading and would have chosen to major in library science but that was not an option. So, I majored in English and added a minor in French.

Early on at college, I learned a valuable lesson about earned privileges. In several of my classes I earned A 's. The instructor could allow an A student to skip the final exam; however, I was fearful of skipping them. I reasoned, "After all, if I really know the material, why shouldn't I demonstrate it in my exam? And, if I don't know it, I should take the exam to learn what my deficiencies are." So, although I had the privilege of skipping some exams, I seldom cashed in on this perk.

During the freshman year, I also discovered that I possessed leadership and organizational skills. We were assigned chemistry with a young instructor who had just completed college. I had not studied chemistry in high school. The subject was completely foreign to me, so I was attentive in class. Sadly, it was Greek to me. The final exam included three questions: State the title of the text book, name the authors, and the publishers. Of the 75 students in that class, four people earned D's; all the rest failed the course. I suspected she gave that shabby exam because she realized she had not adequately taught the course. I began to ask around and found that many of us were dissatisfied. I drafted a petition to the President, and most of us signed it. When Dr. Peters ushered our student delegation into his office, I stated that the course had been inadequately taught, and that the instructor had given that bogus exam to cover her own inadequacies. Dr, Peters said, "These are serious charges from a freshman. But I will investigate the matter." His solution was to assign her to re-teach the course to the whole class. Although she accused me of being the leader, she did not retaliate; instead, we became good friends. That was the hardest course I took during my entire college career, but I passed – with a grade of C. I was never so happy to get a C! And I learned a valuable lesson: when you think you have been wronged, speak up.

Before I enrolled at college, I had always enjoyed mathematics; in fact, I had considered majoring in the subject. A classmate and I agreed to challenge each other for a strong showing in mathematics. We entered class the first day and sat in the front row; we did not want any distractions. Our instructor was the head of the mathematics department, so we expected to learn a lot. His opening comments established the rules for the class: "One third of your grade will be determined by your final exam; one third by written class work, and another third by class participation. Waving your hand to respond will assure you will not be called on. Everyone must remain in his/her assigned seat."

He assigned seats. We were not seated alphabetically; in fact, the only conclusion my friend could reach when the seating arrangement was finished was that all the attractive females, those with fair skin and with long hair were placed on the front row. Our color was a much darker brown, so we were assigned to the back row. We were crest-fallen. We were also intimidated about responding to the questions we did know. I resented that man for a long time; in fact, I formed a mental block about this experience for a long time.

As a sophomore, I felt that I had mastered the routines of college life. My newly gained confidence served me well. My grades began to show consistency and my class participation improved. My professors began to notice me. Two English professors, Dr. Ruth Bartholomew, and Miss Sue Craig invited three of their best English majors to their home for dinner, including me. I was flattered. Both of these women were missionaries who devoted their lives to teaching African and African American students. In fact, when Dr. Bartholomew took her sabbatical, she spent the year teaching in Rhodesia (Zaire). Both women could trace their ancestry back to the Mayflower. I enjoyed their company. Miss Craig had done an informal assessment of our reading ability by having members of the class read out loud. She took notice of how expressively I read. So, before the Christmas holiday she approached me: "Miss Walker, you almost have an A average. Would you like to read three books over vacation and report on them? If successful, you can pull your grade up to solid A."

I accepted the assignment. One of the books was about the life of Louisa May Alcott. When I returned to campus, Miss Craig came to the dormitory that very night to question me about the content. She asked probing and sometimes detailed questions. She was satisfied that I had indeed read the books. So she awarded me a grade of A.

These two white instructors tried to prepare me for the racism and segregation I would face in the real world. Dr. Bartholomew told me that I would have to be a better teacher than a white teacher just to get a chance at being hired. She also shared how the two of them were discriminated against in the white community because they chose to teach African American students. Neither of them had a car, so they had to ride the city bus. One day, on a trip to town, Dr. Bartholomew voluntarily sat in the back of the bus. A white man deliberately stepped on her foot and ground his foot on her toe. It was so painful it brought tears to her eyes. She knew better than to protest, so she meekly apologized for having her foot in his way. He called her a "nigger lover". Sometimes, the women hired me to iron clothes for them. It was obvious that I had no allowance as some of the students had, and I suppose they wanted to help me have money to spend.

Although I did not have a steady beau, on some occasions it was good to have an escort. In my junior year, the class was treated to an event that resembled a high school prom. We were expected to wear formal clothes, and, if possible, we could have an escort. This affair was reserved for upper classmen only. Freshmen and sophomores were only allowed to attend as invited escorts.

A sophomore named William asked if he could escort me to the dinner-dance. I thought there was no harm in that gesture, so I agreed. He looked handsome in his dark suit, and I looked pretty in my long dress. We were seated at the table with the Dean of Women. Dean Gray and I were talking about something that interested us both. We tried to draw William into the conversation. Not knowing anything about the subject he was uncomfortable, so he decided to make a joke. He said, "You know, Odessa, when I look at some people's face, I am thankful for my dog." For a moment, everyone was quiet. Then I looked at him long and hard – and laughed heartily! Others joined me. He blushed and realized that his joke had backfired. He was silent for the remainder of the evening. I enjoyed the whole event, but obviously, our friendship came to an abrupt end.

Whenever I returned home on break from college, I frequently got a ride back to Paine with my best friend's dad, Reverend Thompson. However, after spring break during my junior year, Rev. Thompson was unable to give me a ride. Daddy had to take me back early so he would not miss too much work. Miss Bacon, my play mother lived in Augusta. My parents gave permission for me to spend the week with her. However, instead of taking me to her home, Daddy took me to school to leave most of my baggage. I went in to tell Dean Gray that my parents had given permission for me to stay with Miss Bacon until classes officially started. Dean Gray would have no part of it. "No, I'm sorry, Young Lady, but you must remain on campus." No amount of argument would dissuade her. Finally, I said, "Dean Gray, my daddy is outside waiting to take me to Miss Bacon's house."

She told me to bring my daddy in to meet her. And that's when I noticed! Daddy was unaccustomed to buying clothing for himself. I suppose he was ashamed to wear his work clothes for the trip, and of course, he didn't want to drive a long distance in his dress suit. So, he had bought a pair of pants that must have been two sizes too small! I was so embarrassed for my dad. He could barely walk in those pants. Poor Daddy! There was no sacrifice he wouldn't make for his children.

Dean Gray explained that college rules would not permit me to leave the campus to live with *anyone* in the city, not even Miss Bacon. Daddy said he understood. But I was so disappointed! I had looked forward to staying off campus so I could brag to my roommates when they returned to school. I waved goodbye to Daddy with tears in my eyes. This time my daddy could not rescue me.

During our senior year, three of us young women and I roomed together in the senior suite. My three roommates were Home Economic majors. For their fashion show, when they modeled their own original creations, it was customary to ask a high achieving English major to serve as narrator. That honor was given to me. My reward was a color analysis and a dress made just for me! It was a beige, satin dress made with a draped front. It was beautiful! And it fit perfectly. Was I proud! This event boosted my self-esteem. I had always told myself that clothes were not very important to me, but my sister felt that I was deprived. When I went home on break that year, the high school Home Economics teacher told me that Pearline had made for herself two dresses. They were all she had for herself that year. I was nonplussed. I had accepted the clothes she and Mama were sending me. At one time, I counted thirteen blouses! Her self-sacrifice humbled me. I knew that she profusely disliked sewing. For years after that, I was unable to purchase an item of clothing for myself without feeling guilty. Pearline's explanation was that she thought I should dress as well as the other girls.

46

From my childhood, I refused to lower my eyes and my head when I met white folks. Many white folks would try to stare me down, and would utter nasty remarks. At Paine College, I came to understand that these people acted this way because they felt their sense of white superiority to be threatened by my seeming confident, aloof, and impregnable demeanor.

One day, when I was returning to college after the first semester of my senior year, I had to transfer to another bus in Albany, Ga. I was in a hurry to get on the bus, and struggled with my heavy suitcase. When the announcement was made to reload, I rushed to be first in line. With confidence, I looked the surly white driver straight in the eye. With a snarl he said, "You better git back where you belong, Girl!" I understood that meant to get in line behind all the white folks. I was hurt, but I felt helpless to do anything about the injustice. Suddenly, I missed my dad. These kinds of racist attitudes made me appreciate my dad's protection so much more. He was almost always kind. Very few things annoyed him, except when someone mistreated his children. As I rode in the back of the bus, I decided that when I got a job, I would not return eye for eye when faced with racial bigots.

One other incident stands out in my senior year. Our exams were hand written; we sat in the auditorium for four hours. English majors knew that they were allowed no more than four errors per page on final English exams. There were eight English majors in the class. I observed them studying hard every spare minute. When someone asked why I was not studying the same way, I responded that I had studied hard all along and felt no need to cram. All questions were essay types. You either knew the material or you didn't. I was not surprised that I got one of the highest scores.

Throughout my years at Paine College, attendance at Sunday vesper services and other religious activities were mandatory. I had the opportunity to hear a wide variety of outstanding speakers. Many of them touched my soul. I gained a sense of inner worth and courage to face the racism of the post-war era. I am deeply grateful for the spiritual maturity I achieved as a result of these activities. It was in this setting that I gained an appreciation for hymns of the faith that still stand me in good stead. As my college years came to a close, graduation consumed my attention. The most memorable part of commencement was the speaker: Dr. Benjamin E. Mays. The Dean of Women at Paine, Dean Emma Gray was Dr. Mays' sister-in-law, so he was frequently invited to speak at Paine. He was President of

Morehouse College in Atlanta, a college that had a reputation for molding men. And they did! Morehouse men still stand out in a crowd. To his credit, Dr. Mays had mentored Martin Luther King Jr. Dr. Mays was a great speaker. Some of his remarks seared themselves into my mind; I remember them today. In his challenge to us to make an impact on the world, he closed with this quotation from James Russell Lowell's "The Present Crisis":

"Truth forever on the scaffold, Wrong forever on the throne, -

Yet that scaffold sways the future, and, behind the dim unknown,

Standeth God within the shadows, keeping watch above His own."

As he spoke those words, Dr. Mays raised his arms; every person in that auditorium stood as he ended.

I thank God for the education I received at Paine College. My philosophy for life was born there. Subsequent experiences built on the firm foundation laid at Paine College.

For college graduation, I received some memorable gifts. My friend, Walter Jackson Jr. whom I had accompanied for vocal performances in high school asked me what I wanted for a graduation gift. I requested the sheet music of Vivian Postell's repertoire (She was a singer I had accompanied while in college). I still have that music, even though it is frayed and almost unusable.

My mother gave me a one-month visit to Florida so I could travel with Postell and accompany her as she sang for various performances. My youngest brother was born the same year I graduated, so my mother had her hands full – as she always had. To spare me for a whole month after graduation was quite a gift.

Chapter 18

1951 – 1952: BEGINNING a CAREER

One thing Paine College did not prepare me for was job hunting. I naively thought that with an outstanding college career someone would come looking for me. Surprise! No one did. My parents were unable to give me guidance; however, I decided to make the Georgia State Department of Education aware of my availability. Soon after my registration with the Georgia State Board of Education, I received a letter from a principal in Barnesville, Georgia. He needed a high school English teacher. Was I interested? I thought, " Where in the state is Barnesville! " I soon discovered where it was and how I would have to get there: by bus.

Before leaving home, however, I felt I needed to help Daddy. Poor Daddy! With eight children still at home, we had long outgrown our house. It was so important to him that we attend college that he had sacrificed family comfort for us. I began to lobby for a bigger house. Daddy said, "Dessa Ree, I can't pay a house note and your sister's tuition at the same time." My sister, Pearline had completed two years at Florida A&M University on a partial scholarship. Daddy was really struggling. Now, I felt it was my time to "step up to the plate." "Daddy, I'll pay Pearline's tuition, and you can pay for the house."

Randy and I had declared our love for each other before we finished high school and had planned to discuss marriage after I graduated from college. He delayed his own entrance into college because he joined the military. Now, with my new financial obligation it was necessary to postpone marriage again. I also told him that I thought it was only fair that he should not be married while in college; after all, he might meet someone he wanted to marry more than me. He agreed and said, "I really want to be able to work and support my family when we get married." So, for the first two years after I graduated, I sent Pearline's tuition money every month. That was quite a sacrifice. After I paid my rent and bought groceries there was barely enough to pay her tuition. But I kept my promise to Daddy, who had always said we should help each other.

49

The principal of Barnesville High School and his wife met me at the bus station, and took me to a home where they had secured lodging for me. The Demon family treated me like a member of the family. Mrs. Demon was a grade-school teacher and helped orient me to the school system. This family had built an attached apartment to their home for the purpose of renting to teachers. The arrangement was good; but my roommate was not an ideal match. She had been married and divorced. Her life experiences were too advanced for me. I decided to share the living quarters and expense, knowing that we were not social equals.

My first teaching assignment challenged me. I was only twenty years old when I started teaching. I contracted to teach two English classes and one French class. My students were more like my social equals; in fact, five of my students were older than I was. They were veterans who had returned to school to complete their education after serving in the military. What a Godsend they were! There were three teen-aged boys in one of my English classes who challenged my authority. We read a poem by Edgar Allen Poe, and I asked each student to create a cryptogram, a coded message. These boys would have no part of it. Two of the veterans, Walter, and M.C. came to my defense. Walter said, "Boy! Did Miss Walker tell you to do something? You better sit yourself down and I'd better not hear another word from you!"

The boys got the message! But they resented it. During the last week before the Christmas holiday break, I discovered that my coat had been slashed down the back. The principal called the police. After a few questions from me and some of the students, it was revealed that these three boys had slashed my coat to get even with me. It was a hardship on their parents to pay for the damage; it was harder on the boys-literally. Their dads took them to the woodshed. During the next semester, I called on their parents and visited with them in their homes in an attempt to establish more positive relationships with the families and to end the year on a positive note. I assigned the boys important tasks like cleaning the chalkboards and assuming responsibility for making and maintaining a fire in the wood stove. They responded positively to the extra attention.

Some students were very motivated. I voluntarily organized a group of girls to form a singing quintet. I purchased yard goods and made costumes for them. I sewed a brown skirt to go with a beige blouse; a royal blue skirt went with a light blue blouse. All of the skirts and blouses were colors that complimented each other. The girls were proud to wear them. I taught them several Duke Ellington songs. After a school performance, we took our show on the road presenting it at a variety of churches and social clubs in the surrounding communities. I accompanied them on the piano and we were well received.

I also served as senior class advisor, helping the class to decide on a gift for the school. After much debate, they chose to donate a large glass case to display the trophies won by the boys' and girls' basketball teams. From my homeroom class of 20 + students, six attended college. Some friendships lasted for years. I felt very good that year; being a high school teacher was very rewarding.

At the end of my first year of teaching, I needed to return to college to get a teacher's certificate in order to teach at the high school level. My undergraduate education training had been at the elementary level. I discovered that the Georgia Board of Education did not allow African Americans to attend graduate school at white state universities; instead, our expenses were covered if we attended an African American graduate school. I took three courses at Atlanta University the summer of 1952 to qualify as a certified high school teacher.

5 Generations
Aunt Faustine Hall
(daddy's maternal aunt) seated.
Twins: Kymberley & Kisha Riggins,
Anderson, Sr., Odessa & Douglas Hooker

Daddy & Mama
1975

Daddy & Mama
1984

addy with great granddaughter,
Nikki Riggins
1982

Anderson, Jr. joking
with Daddy & Mama
1984

Daddy with granddaughter,
Letitia Ensley
1985

Aisha with her daddy,
Kenneth and her Granddaddy Anderson

front view   side view

2nd home purchased by Daddy and Mama 815 Third Ave. N.W. Moultrie, GA.

1st. row: Odessa, Pearline, Betty
2nd. row: Anderson, Jr., Freddie, Kenneth, Andrea
3rd. row: Woodrow , Oreatha
March 1998

1st. row: Anderson, Jr. and Betty
2nd. row: Odessa and Pearline

Part Two: Personal Life as Wife and Parent

1953 – 1999

Chapter 19

1953: MARRIAGE to CHILDHOOD SWEETHEART

I taught at Barnesville High School from 1951 to 1953. At the end of my second year of work there, Pearline finished college at Florida A&M University. My obligation to pay her tuition ended. Anticipating her graduation, Randy and I decided to marry. He was still a junior at South Carolina State University. Furthermore, Randy insisted that he had spent three years in the military and had dated many women, but he still wanted to marry me. We dismissed the idea of a church wedding because of insufficient funds.

While at home for Christmas in 1952 he gave me his fraternity pin to wear until he could replace it with a wedding ring, and we secured a marriage license. We had postponed our marriage for too long. The minister who we wanted to perform the ceremony, Rev. Thompson was out of town, and would not return before we had to leave Moultrie. So, we decided to postpone the wedding -again - until winter break in January.

I began to eagerly anticipate our marriage. We had patiently waited for more than eight years. However, the week before it was time to return home for the wedding, I came down with a bad flu. I tried to ignore my illness because I wanted to go home to get married. My principal insisted that I see a doctor. The idea was foreign to me. I was not accustomed to seeing a doctor except for emergencies. The doctor admonished me and recommended that I stay in bed for at least a week. I protested, "I have to go home this weekend; I'm supposed to get married!" The doctor said, "I'm sure your intended will understand. Anyway, you don't want to go home and give him the flu."

That night I called Randy to tell him what the doctor had said. "Our license will expire in thirty days. I'll come to you. Don't worry." Randy came to Barnesville. I secured a room for him with a family down the street. On January 24, 1953, we married.

My best friend at the school acted as my bridesmaid. Sallie Clare came to the apartment and helped me get dressed. The powder blue suit I had chosen to wear did not help me feel stronger. That weekend it rained cats and dogs! The street was so muddy, Randy had to roll up his pants legs and walk in his bare feet to the Demon's house. When he arrived, he washed his feet and put his socks and shoes on. When Rev. Wilson arrived at the Demons' house, Sallie Clare literally helped me stand for the ceremony; I was really sick. After the ceremony, Sallie Clare helped me prepare our wedding dinner. We cooked roast beef, corn on the cob, and other vegetables. For dessert, I made a lemon meringue pie. Randy ate so heartily, I began to feel better just watching him eat. He raved about the pie. "I have a wife who is not only pretty, but she can cook, too," he chuckled.

What may have appeared to be an unplanned marriage in January caused my principal to suspect that we had married in mid-year because I was pregnant. He decided not to renew my contract at the end of the year. Oblivious of Mr. Roberts' thoughts, Randy and I were happy. He stayed in Barnesville for about a week. As I regained my strength, we walked through the neighborhood and took pictures. We also visited the school where he met teachers and students. Then he returned to South Carolina State to finish his degree in Physical Education. I returned to work.

My job was important to me, and I performed my duties faithfully. One day, without prior notice, the principal, Mr. Roberts sent word that all the teachers should meet on the front steps of the school. I decided I would go when the class was over. He sent word that I was to come immediately! I couldn't imagine what was more important than teaching my class, since there was no one to supervise the students. Surely he knew that. Reluctantly, I left the students with an assignment and went to meet the principal on the front steps. I was surprised to learn that the superintendent was there with a photographer. He wanted a picture of the staff. I couldn't believe it! Couldn't this be done at a time when we were not engaged with our classes? To show my resentment, I stood on the top row (where I was directed to go) but I stood apart from the group. The superintendent said to the principal, "Bob, tell that girl up there to move in closer to the group." The principal said, gesturing with his hand, "Miss Walker, move more to your right." I refused to move. When he ordered me to move in closer the second time, I did so resentfully, and refused to smile.

After school that day, I was called to the principal's office, and lectured soundly. "Don't you know that that was the superintendent?

Aren't you aware that your attitude could cost you your job? What would your daddy say if he knew what you did?" I protested, "The superintendent of all people should know better than to interrupt classes and demand a photograph of all the teachers during the school day! Surely, as the principal you could have asked him to get the picture at a more suitable time." "But Miss Walker, that was the *Superintendent!*"

This incident confirmed his decision not to renew my contract. On the last day of school he called me into his office and told me that I was a very good teacher; but because I was pregnant, that would render me ineligible to work the following year. Mr. Roberts couldn't have been more wrong. When we returned home for the summer, we were Mr. and Mrs. Homer Randolph Hooker. For the first time we were alone in our own place. Two of our friends were moving, because of a military re-assignment. O. C and Marjorie McKinney rented us their apartment. During the summer of 1953, Randy took a summer job before reporting for duty in the Army Reserves. Then he returned to South Carolina State University to complete his senior year. Before he returned to school, I was pregnant. We had been living with his mother when the new school year began. After he left, I lived with my parents while awaiting the birth of our first child.

Chapter 20

1954: THE BIRTH of OUR FIRST BORN SON

Our first born son was already nearly two weeks overdue. It was March 31, 1954. It was a bright sunny day, and I busied myself by painting mama's living and dining rooms. I was exhausted and went to bed early. Before getting into bed, I got down on my knees and prayed, "Lord, please let my baby come tonight. I don't want him to be born on April Fools' Day." Immediately, I felt the first labor pain. I called to Daddy, "I think it's time to go to the hospital."
He got on the phone and called the doctor, who told him to time the pains and take me to the hospital when they were five minutes apart. I had already packed my bags, so I used the time to get dressed. Daddy drove me to Vereen Memorial Hospital, but he was not allowed to accompany me. I was surprised by the lack of care I was given. I was strapped to a hospital bed and left alone. I struggled, "Please don't strap me down!"

It was no use. The staff completely ignored me. I was left alone in the room for what seemed like hours. They gave me no pain medication. I couldn't imagine they would have treated a white woman that way. Shortly before midnight, Dr. McCoy came and delivered the baby.

Randy and I had arrived at a name for the baby. He had never liked his own name. When we were seniors in high school, many of our classmates wanted at least three names. At that time, Randy had chosen to add the middle name 'Randolph'; thus his name became Homer Randolph Hooker. Now my suggestion was to name our son for his daddy. Randy stated, "My son can carry his *own* name. He does not need to rely on being a junior."

Douglas Randolf Hooker was born before midnight March 31, 1954. The hospital policy did not allow Black mothers to stay overnight. After the delivery, my older brother, Anderson Jr. took Doug and me home. Randy met his three-weeks-old son for the first time when he returned home for Easter break. I made it a point to send a birth announcement to my former principal, Mr. Roberts, so he could see that he had been wrong about his reason for not renewing my teaching contract.

Randy came home with a beautiful Easter card for my mother. I was hurt. "Why didn't you bring a card for me?" His excuse was, "You know this is my first time to have a mother-in-law." "Do you mean this is not your first time to have a wife?"

He enjoyed watching and holding his new son. He proudly wheeled Doug to visit with his mother. A short time later, I heard a baby screaming at the top of its lungs. Randy and Doug were returning from their visit. Doug was hungry and needed a change of diaper. He conveyed these messages the only way that he knew how. As I took him from his daddy and consoled him, Randy chuckled, "The next time I take you someplace, you will be cutting steak with a knife."

After the Easter break, Randy returned to South Carolina State. In order to complete his degree, he enrolled in summer classes. He graduated August 1954. During that summer, I accepted a job as an Avon salesperson. This job allowed me to breast feed our son and set my own work schedule. My mother-in-law thought it was shameful that my husband was finishing school while I tried to support Doug and me. I disagreed. "Mama, when he gets his degree he will have a better chance at finding a good job."

Doug and I did not attend Randy's graduation. However, he was hired immediately by the principal of Whittemore High School in Conway, South Carolina to teach science and coach football and basketball. He was handed the keys to the new gymnasium. The baby and I waited until Randy found housing, then we joined him. We traveled by bus to Conway, South Carolina. When we arrived, Randy was not there to meet us. I asked where the school was located. A white truck driver was going our way and gave us a lift. It was necessary to stop at one point so I could change Doug's diaper. The truck driver didn't seem to mind waiting. I thought that was unusually kind and very thoughtful. He refused to accept money for helping us.

Randy had rented a house from a licensed practical nurse who worked in other people's home on the premises and lived with them. She rented her house out to teachers. She specified teachers because they were trustworthy and could pay the rent! The house was furnished. She had purchased a gas burning stove for our convenience. There were three bedrooms, a living room, and a kitchen. But no indoor plumbing! The house had a front and back porch. We got our water from a pump, and there was a toilet on the back porch with a septic tank. Mrs. Gee came every month to collect the rent from "Mistah Hook." She was of Gullah ancestry and orientation; she did business only with the man of the house. She was polite to me, but talked only with Randy about business.

As we set up our new household I told Randy I wanted to stay home with the baby, but he strongly urged me to work. A few days later, Randy's principal told me he had an opening for an English teacher. I accepted the job. I knew no one in this rural community so I walked through the streets of the town with Doug in the stroller in search of a baby sitter. To my relief, I found one. The young woman who took the job was a gem! Sarah had just graduated from high school and needed a job. She loved our baby dearly and took excellent care of him. She came to work on her own. We could not pick her up because we had no car yet. The school was located less than a mile from our home, so we walked to and from school. Sarah gladly stayed with Doug until we got home from work. He was her living doll baby; she kept him spotless. I appreciated her diligence, but he was a boy. He needed to play in the dirt. Our yards were covered with dirt; so were the roads. So, the first thing I did when I got home from work at 3:30 p.m. was to take him outside to play in the yard. After a half-hour we went inside and I prepared to make dinner. He enjoyed a regular ritual. First, he would open the stove and take out every pot and pan, bang them on the floor, then look at me as if to say, "Look, Mommy. Look what I did!" I smiled indulgently. His next stop was in the living room. There was a table with shelves underneath. Mrs. Gee had books on the shelves. Doug methodically took them off the shelves, one at a time. Then he looked around for his next exploratory task. He enjoyed shredding paper, so I gave him alternately newspaper and toilet paper. He squealed with delight. After he finished his rounds, I was finished with dinner. Following his feeding, bath, and story time, he was ready for bed.

His adjustment to this new place took time. He cried for me to stay with him. After a few nights of this, I knew I had to help him learn to go to sleep on his own. His favorite toy was an elephant named Homer. I gave him Homer and kissed him goodnight. But, he would cry for me to stay with him. I knew that he had to learn to go to sleep on his own. So, I placed a quilt over the window to muffle his crying and allowed him to cry for twenty minutes one night. It broke my heart, but it also broke his crying for me at bedtime. Sometimes, Randy came home in time for dinner. On those occasions, he played with Doug and sometimes put him to bed.

During our first year in Conway, the community encountered a hurricane: Hurricane Hazel. We were aware of the heavy rain, but we had no radio or television, so were unaware of the severity of the storm. During the night, a windowpane was blown out in Doug's room. The next morning, we got up and dressed for work. Randy said, "I'll go first to see if there is school today. If I don't come back, you'll know to come on." He took the umbrella and left by the back door. Almost immediately he returned - soaking wet. He exclaimed, "Our neighbors' porch roof is in our back yard!"

That was when we discovered the severity of the storm. There was no electricity for two weeks. Trees were down in the roads, and the storm damaged many houses. The only damage we sustained was the missing windowpane in Doug's room. Randy put cardboard in the space to replace it temporarily. With no electric power, that gas burning stove proved to be a lifesaver. I could cook, and we could heat water for a bath. Doug was in diapers. I could wash his diapers and boil them on the stove.

Life in the community returned to normal after about three weeks. School had been suspended, but as soon as the damage was repaired, we went back to work.

Chapter 21

1955: MARRIAGE BREAKUP

and MOVING FAR AWAY FROM HOME

Increasingly, Randy came home late after school, well after dinner. He practiced with the teams after school; occasionally, the teams traveled to play at other schools. That was acceptable. But, I began to feel that he preferred to find other excuses to stay away from home unnecessarily. One day I suggested that we ask Sarah to stay with Doug so I could go with him to some of the games. "No, Dess, you will get home too late. With your workload and the baby, you need to get all the rest you can." Some of the teachers with whom we worked had begun to be friendly with us. Several times we were invited to go to Myrtle Beach to catch crabs after school. I was delighted. Many of the teachers were unmarried, and were free to attend games and other activities. Occasionally there was a social gathering of the teachers.

At one such gathering, I mixed with some of the faculty with whom I had little occasion to socialize. One woman was a standup comic. She had all of us laughing. I didn't notice where my husband was, but later when we got home, he accused me of enjoying jokes at someone's expense. I didn't know what he was talking about. This woman was telling jokes about how poor she and her husband had been when they were first married. She talked about how she used baking powder to stretch the eggs so they could both eat one egg. There were several more jokes like that, but we were not laughing at anyone in particular. One night, two of the teachers invited us to dinner at their apartment. It was a lovely evening. I was starved for social life and adult conversation. They played records and we danced. It was so enjoyable. One of them said, "You should hire a baby sitter and come to some of the games. The teams are good, and you need to see what kind of job your husband is doing as coach."

I thought attending a game was a good idea. Randy did not! Then I began to notice what I perceived as hostility toward me from another teacher at the school. So, I decided I would attend the next game away from home. My husband was adamant: "No, you should not go!" Resentfully, I stayed home.

66

That night, I waited up for him. When he came home well after midnight I greeted him at the door. He pushed me away, and announced that he was leaving us the next day! I was dumbfounded. He refused to discuss anything with me. Instead, he began to pack his clothes. "You owe me an explanation; I want some answers."

Randy gave me the silent treatment. Then I began to plead with him. "What do you expect Doug and me to do? We know no one here. How will we manage by ourselves? What should we do?" "I don't know!" " What have we done? Where are you going?" Suddenly, he slapped me in the face. I was crushed. I knew then that I should not try to restrain him further.

Although we had been married since January 1953 we had only been living together as a family since September of 1954; he left us in February of 1955. He did not finish his first year's teaching contract. I went to work the next day, but I was in a daze. The faculty was buzzing. An older woman, chairman of the English department befriended me. She helped me sort out my next steps. That weekend, I took Doug home to Georgia to stay with my parents. I came back to work; I had to finish my contract obligations. I moved in with the family of my friend from the English department. They were so kind. To distract myself and to fill my loneliness for my baby and my husband, I joined a creative dance group at the school. That helped me so much! It had been a long time since I participated in creative dancing. I poured myself into work and play. By the end of the year, I had paid all the bills my husband left me. I took a bus and went home to Georgia to see my baby! He was 11 months old when his daddy left; four months had passed since I had seen him last. I wondered, "Will he remember me?" Daddy picked me up at the bus station. As we pulled up to the house, I saw that Doug was playing with my youngest brother, Woodrow. Mama called, "Doug, your mother is here."

Doug squealed and ran to me. My heart was pounding as I put my arms around him. I was so relieved that he remembered me. We resumed our lives. I decided to move away from my parents; I had a need to prove that I could take care of Doug and myself. And, I didn't want to explain to friends and family what had happened between Randy and me.

In August of 1955, Doug and I moved to Cincinnati to live with my maternal grandmother until I could get on my feet again. Cincinnati was not strange to me. I had spent a summer in Cincinnati when I was fourteen. Many members of my mother's family lived there. In fact, my mother had once attended Stowe School in Cincinnati.

All my family welcomed me to Cincinnati. My Uncle Joe was pastor of Peoples Tabernacle Baptist Church, which I began attending, and I took a job playing the piano for the choir. When Doug and I were settled in, suddenly Randy reappeared at the door. "Dess, I am so sorry about leaving you and the baby; it was a stupid thing to do. May I please come back?"

Chapter 22

1957 – 1960: RECONCILLIATION and THREE MORE CHILDREN

I was eager to have the family together, so Randy joined us in Cincinnati. We had to find our own apartment. My grandmother would get into trouble with the housing authority if the three of us stayed too long with her. While looking for a place to live, we moved in with Aunt Teddy. Uncle Will found work for Randy at the tannery where he worked. My family welcomed Randy joyfully; they too wanted our marriage to work.

Three months later we moved into the apartment next door to Aunt Teddy who was very helpful. We had not established any credit, so she co-signed for our first furniture. We resumed life as a family. Randy and I talked often about what had caused him to leave us. He admitted to having had an affair with a woman whom he had known in college. She came to work at the same high school. They were thrown together again and soon they were entangled in an affair. Randy said, "When she told me she was pregnant, I panicked. The only thing I could think to do was leave before word of the affair got out in the community. Later, I learned she was not pregnant. She just wanted to break up our marriage. As soon as I realized this, I wanted to try to mend our marriage." I was deeply hurt, but I pledged to forgive him and move on with our lives.

It was time to start thinking about going to work. I wrote to the Ohio State Department of Education and received a teaching certificate that certified me to teach high school English. Durling the interview with the personnel director, I was asked "Who got this certificate for you?" "I did. I wrote and requested it, and they sent it to me." "Well, you weren't supposed to get it; we do that ourselves. Anyway, there are no vacancies for which you qualify."

Unknown to me, it was the practice of the Cincinnati Board of Education not to hire African American English teachers, particularly ones from the South. I was sent to talk with another person in personnel. "Let me explain how we operate in Cincinnati. As a teacher new to the system, we encourage you to begin as a substitute teacher."

I didn't mind that, however, when she explained how the system worked, I realized I might not work regularly. Nevertheless, I agreed to work as a substitute teacher. Being a substitute teacher was a traumatic experience. I didn't have a car, and I didn't know my way around Cincinnati. Each assignment was at a different school. After I received a call - early in the morning - I had to get Doug ready to leave him with my grandmother. That required a bus trip. Then, I had to ride a second bus to get to school and was almost always late! After the fourth such experience, I withdrew my name from the substitute teacher pool.

I began looking for other work. For the first time in my life I was told that I was overqualified. What on earth did that mean? I finally worked as a domestic. Several of my aunts worked as domestics so they helped me find jobs. One woman for whom I worked discovered that I was an English teacher. She wanted me to tutor her daughter. I refused. "No, that was not a part of the agreement." It was stressful trying to find baby-sitting but I was grateful for any kind of work. However, I soon discovered daily pay of $7.00 plus bus fare could not pay a baby sitter; it was necessary to depend on family members to help me.

Soon, I was pregnant again. During the pregnancy, I had to find a doctor for prenatal care. The medical association recommended two doctors whose practice was near our residence; it was easy to get to their offices on the bus line. Our first daughter Melanie was born August 22, 1957 at the Deaconess Hospital. Her birth caused curiosity among the hospital personnel. Deaconess Hospital had just recently begun to admit African Americans. I surmised that Melanie might have been the first African American baby many of the hospital staff had seen. She looked perfectly normal to us, but to someone who had never seen a new African American baby, her color and hair texture might have seemed strange. Melanie Ann Hooker was beautiful! She was very fair and her hair (lots of it!) was straight. Her dad called her his live doll baby. Both of her parents were brown. Many white folks still do not realize that in the African American race one can see skin color ranging from white (pink) to ebony, and eye colors including blue and green. My maternal biological grandmother was part Cherokee. My grandfather was born to his light skinned mother and her white master. Granddaddy Hill had green eyes and curly hair.

The director of nursing visited with me two or three times during my five-day stay in the hospital. I didn't think this was unusual. I had taken Doug's picture with me to the hospital. "Oh, I see you brought your family with you. I think that's nice." I thought she was making conversation, but when Randy came to visit us, he said, "Did you know they didn't want to allow me to visit you?" "Why?" "They said I was not the baby's daddy." "What did they mean by that?" "I don't know, but I reassured them that I am her daddy and you are my wife." I dismissed the whole thing. On his next visit, Randy said, "I had to present evidence to show that I am entitled to visit you and Melanie." We laughed.

Mama came from Moultrie to help out while I was in the hospital. Melanie was welcomed enthusiastically by her brother; Doug had been told he would have a baby sister. He watched her closely when we came home. It occurred to me that he expected her to play with him right away. After watching her for a few days, he lost interest in her as a playmate. He said, "Mother, all Baby Sister can do is eat and sleep and cry." He enjoyed helping with her bath, (he bathed his baby doll when I bathed Mel). But he soon returned to play with his buddies downstairs. Sometimes when she cried, he said, "Mother, baby sister is crying; she wants to eat."

Randy and Doug enjoyed some activities together at this time. Snow was new for both of them, so they played together in the snow – building snowmen and having snowball fights. Later that spring I watched them as they tried to launch a kite. They were like two boys when the kite finally took off.

As our family grew, we needed a larger apartment. Neither Randy nor I had experienced apartment living before, except at college. As the children began to run around and play, the neighbors living underneath us complained of the noise. It was necessary to let them play in their socks. This was hard on their white socks and harder on mom when I had to wash them.

I again became pregnant a few months after Melanie was born; but Randy left us when I was seven months pregnant with David. This time, I was better prepared emotionally and socially. Many relatives were nearby to offer support. I moved in with Uncle Joe and Aunt Edna and their family.

71

Chapter 23

1958: A FAITH -STRETCHING EXPERIENCE

David Anderson Hooker was born October 15, 1958. I went to the hospital alone. At dismissal time the doctor asked who was going to take me home. I said I'd get a taxicab. "You will not." He picked up the telephone and called the police chief. "Sir, my name is Dr. Bassette. The wife of one of your officers has given birth to their child. Would you please allow Officer Hooker to come and take his wife and child home?" Randy picked us up and grudgingly took us to Pearline's house.

I stayed there eleven weeks until David was old enough to travel by bus. Then I took all three children to my parent's home in Georgia. I had not told my parents about our separation. Randy wanted to keep up appearances, so he sent money to us. Again, however, he sent the amount he wanted when he wanted to send it. I saved every penny. As soon as I had saved enough money, I was ready to bring the children back to Cincinnati. It was necessary to be near him to insure that he sent the amount the courts had ordered. And I was hopeful that he would come to his senses and act like a responsible head of the household. I left Doug with my parents. Melanie, David, and I came back on the train. Randy refused to meet us. I called a friend who lived in a building where we had once lived. Mrs. Holt told me to bring the children to her apartment. She was very good to us, but I wanted to get our own place. So I went to work part-time at a department store. A girl in the neighborhood baby-sat the children. I only worked half-days. As soon as I got home, I gave immediate attention to the children. Everyday, after dinner, I took them for a walk in the neighborhood. The area did not lend itself to allowing them to play outside. After our walk, we'd come home, go through the bedtime routines, and I'd put them to bed. I insisted that Randy help support our children; he was just as insistent that he would not.

Mrs. Holt was patient with us but she showed signs of wanting us to move on. One morning before she left for work, she disconnected her television set. I accepted that action as a message that she didn't want the children to watch TV all morning. There was a small fenced in area in the back of the building, but it needed to be cleaned up if

72

the children were to play there. So I cleaned it up and allowed them to play outside. It was a tough neighborhood, so I only allowed them to play outside when I was at home.

I was working part-time; it was difficult to make ends meet. On one occasion our food supply was completely depleted. In my morning meditation I had read that God will take care of you, if you have faith. Here was my chance to put my faith to work. I gave the children breakfast and put them out to play. Then I prayed, "Lord, you know everything; You know we have no more food left. I'm trusting You for provision." Miracle of miracles: the children did not come in to ask for lunch! God had satisfied the children's hunger need. As the day wore on, it was getting near time to start preparing dinner, but there was nothing to prepare. Then there was a knock on the door. It was my sister, Pearline- with two bags of groceries! "Hi Guys! Aunt Jessie couldn't work today; she asked me to go in her place. I thought you might need some food." How could she have known? I had not told my family how we were faring. But God knew, and He sent my sister Pearline as answer to my prayer. I marvel at His grace!

Randy knew where we lived, but he was still angry with me, so he refused to visit the children. By now, they seldom asked for him. School started again in the fall. The baby-sitter had to return to school. In order to continue working, it was necessary to make arrangements for someone to supervise the children. Again, my family came to my rescue. One day, as I was returning home on the bus, I became ill. I stopped at Dr. Bassette's office. He examined me and sent me to see a specialist. Surgery was needed to remove painful hemorrhoids.

An aunt's sister, Peggy, and her husband took the children and me in. While I was in the hospital, the family took care of the children. After I left the hospital, I went back to live with Peggy and her family. Melanie stayed with me, but David was left with Aunt Eunice. I was forbidden to lift him. He was only 10 months old; he had learned to walk quite early, and was an active child. Aunt Eunice had a baby who was the same age as David. It broke my heart to be separated from him at this time in his development. The emotional strain was almost unbearable. Melanie and I would walk over to visit with David every day. Because he was so active, and because my aunt could not handle him and her own baby, she kept David confined to a playpen. When Melanie and I arrived, he was allowed out of the playpen. I would sit in a chair at the kitchen table, and he was placed on my lap. We would snuggle together for a few minutes. He was so happy to see his mother. I fed him dinner. Then he wanted to get down and play with his sister. We would visit with him for about two hours. I dressed David for bed, and then Melanie and I would have to go back to Peggy's. The look in David's eyes brought tears to my eyes. He seemed to say, "Why are you leaving me?" He developed dark rings under his eyes. The circumstances were tearing me apart. Every day as we walked back to our place, I wept silently. Melanie asked, "Why are you crying, Mommy?" Both of them were too young to understand what was happening.

One bright sunny Sunday morning my heart was so heavy, but I knew God had not deserted me. I left Melanie with Peggy and I went to church alone. The minister invited visitors to participate in the services any way they chose. I was moved to walk up and join the choir. My spirits were lifted as I sang with them. I prayed, "Dear Lord, let me and my children be together, and let us to have our own home!"

Randy suddenly had a change of heart. He found an apartment and decided to reunite the family. Doug had turned five; it was time for him attend school. I went back to Georgia to bring him home; he was enrolled in kindergarten for 1/2 year. He did well, though, and the next year, he went to first grade. The school was located less that one block from our apartment, but I would not allow him to walk to school alone. My sister and I decided that she would keep David and Melanie engaged on the telephone while I walked Doug to school. I called Auntie Pearl and allowed Melanie and David to talk with her until I got back. This arrangement was short-lived. Melanie and David soon lost interest in talking on the telephone, and found other things in the house to interest them. Finally, I had to take them with me; they enjoyed walking Dougie to school. Before too long, I could stand outside and watch him as he walked to the corner. The crossing guard was on duty to see him safely across the street.

Because of the proximity of their ages, Melanie and David taxed my ingenuity. They got into a lot of mischief – together. One day after we returned from the doctor's office where they had been taken for routine checkups and shots, I was tired. I took an aspirin and went into my bedroom to change clothes and get ready to prepare dinner. They were in the kitchen, I thought. One of them had spotted the bottle of aspirins on the table, had opened it, and had consumed the whole bottle! I panicked. When I asked who had taken the aspirin, they pointed at each other. I called someone and we were taken to the emergency room at Children's Hospital. Both their stomachs were pumped. The doctor assured me they would be fine. Even today, I do not keep aspirin in my home.

David provided us many visits to the emergency room. At another time when we returned home from a tiring outing, I went to the kitchen to make a cup of tea. After a few minutes Randy and I heard a bloodcurdling scream. David had tried to reach the boiling pot of water, had overturned it, and the hot water scalded his back! After this emergency room visit, the doctor tried to comfort me. "Mrs. Hooker, when you have a child like David, sometimes it is necessary to turn your head and pray." How prophetic! During his growing up years, I spent a lot of time in prayer that was prompted by David's curiosity.

In 1960, I became pregnant again. And, Randy left us again. This time he went a little further; he filed for divorce. In court, the judge asked, "Mr. Hooker, you say you want a divorce on the grounds of incompatibility?" "Yes, Your Honor." "You say you and your wife have three children, and she's pregnant. Is this your child she is carrying?" "Yes, Your Honor." "I can't grant you a divorce while your wife is pregnant."Then the judge asked me, "Mrs. Hooker, do you want a divorce?" "No, sir." "I'm sorry, Mr. Hooker. You come back after the baby comes and we will discuss it again."

Randy was frustrated. I was furious! My eyes were opened and my heart hardened. Outside the courtroom, I said to him, "You used me! You'll never do it again!" I began to make plans to grant him the divorce. The children and I would get along without him. The courts ordered Randy to send us money each month; he resented this bitterly. To get back at me, he refused to visit the children. I was heartbroken when they asked, "Mommy, where is Daddy?" Whenever he sent money, he withheld a part of it. Because the amount withheld was small, I felt he did this to spite me. I decided to fight back. I made an appointment to see the chief of police and request his intervention.

Visiting the police office took a lot of courage: I knew how poorly African Americans were regarded, but I needed help. I was ushered into a spacious office and directed to sit a distance across the room. The police chief asked me what I wanted. I told him that one of his

75

officers had been ordered by the courts to pay support for our children, but the officer did not send the money in a timely fashion, and when he sent it, he withheld a portion of what he was supposed to send.

The chief picked up his telephone. "Send Officer Hooker to my office immediately." Randy came in and faced the chief. "Officer, is this woman your wife?" "Yes, Sir." The police chief continued "Your wife has accused you of failing to comply with the court's orders concerning support payments. Officer, I will not have a policeman on this force who does not support his family. If your wife comes back with this complaint again, I will personally take your keys and lock you in one of the cells downstairs."

Randy was furious! He accused me of trying to make him lose his job. I looked him straight in the eye. "If you lose your job, it will be your own fault. If you send the money that the courts ordered, you will not hear from me again." From that time forward, for a long time, he wore dark glasses. He refused to visit the children or any of my family. He accused them of taking my side against him. He enjoyed portraying himself as the victim. He never acknowledged the harm he inflicted on the family.

Because he refused to pay the rent, we were evicted from the apartment. Our furniture was set out on the street. The only furniture we could salvage was the wrought iron beds. The children and I again went to live with Uncle Joe and his family. Aunt Edna accepted my services as family cook. The children didn't notice too often that their daddy didn't visit. The summer weather was quite helpful. After breakfast, I would take them to the park to play. We would come back to my uncle's home for lunch. While they napped, I cooked dinner. After dinner, I would sometimes take them for another walk. Then it was time for bath and bed.

I couldn't find housing for the money Randy was sending us. I applied for public housing, but we were on a long waiting list. I needed someplace to take the children before the baby arrived. It was necessary to ask Randy's superior for help again. The captain of District Four cut through the red tape, and we moved into the Lincoln Court Housing Project, not too far from my grandmother and Aunt Mildred. They helped me a lot. Aunt Mildred was a master at making

76

meals with little money, and she taught me a lot about wholesome meal preparation. I learned to mix reconstituted powdered milk with whole fresh milk. This milk drink was wholesome for the children, and they could get their daily allotment. I could drink milk, too. Our meals were often meatless, but nourishing nevertheless. My groceries were bulk purchases that were long lasting; i.e. potatoes, carrots, apples, dried fruits, dried beans, etc. I became an expert at cooking black-eyed peas, seasoned with ham hock and served with corn bread. Every Wednesday, I cleaned out the refrigerator and used all the leftovers to make "Hooker Stew". Then, I used a $0.25 can of Comstock apples to make an apple pie for dessert. We could not afford frills like fast foods, candies, or soda pop. The food we ate was more nourishing than fast foods.

But our living conditions troubled me. The concrete courtyard was absolutely no place for my children to play. Once I let Doug go out there. I heard what sounded like a child's head crack, and crying followed. I recognized the cry of my son. From that time on, I took them over to the park every day from 4:00 until 5:00 to play in the grass. They were no longer allowed to play in the concrete courtyard.

There were other problems. The noise level in the projects at night was nerve wracking. We did not have air-conditioning. Some of the neighbors gambled and used foul language. This frightened me. The police never came in response to calls unless someone was murdered. And there were the roaches! I had never seen so many roaches. I declared war on them; they could not live with my children! When the housing inspectors came, they commended me for my housekeeping.

The children could not have a pet, so we adopted the pigeons that landed on the window ledge. I composed songs for them to sing about the pigeons. Every morning, before I helped them dress for breakfast, I spent time alone with Bible reading and meditating. God guided me through His Word. I gained courage to face whatever happened. And, several things did happen to stretch my faith. Each day, I talked with God about our circumstances. "Lord, you own all the houses in the world. Please help me get one for my children and me."

Later that summer, Daddy sent Mama to see how we were faring. He wanted me to come back to Moultrie, Georgia; he would build for the children and me a house on the lot adjoining their home. I assured him that I appreciated what he wanted to do, but felt the children were my responsibility. Mama said he told her to come because he didn't trust himself to confront my husband. Mama stayed with us as long as she could. She wanted to stay to help me after the baby came, but it was necessary for her to return home before Margaret was born. "I'll tell your daddy that you are doing as well as we are. You are calm, make good plans, and the children are well organized. I trust God to take care of you all."

One day, as I was washing dishes, I was talking to God as usual. I was telling Him what kind of house I wanted for the children and why: "They are unable to play outside in that concrete courtyard. Would You help us find a house with grass and trees? And can we live in a neighborhood where there is a good school? You promised to reward us for small faith. I have already witnessed Your promise that You will not forsake the righteous, and [my] children will not have to beg for bread. Thank You for caring for us and for loving us."

The next day, as I was praying about the need for a house, I was prompted to go downtown. I had no idea where I was being directed to go but I asked Aunt Mildred to watch the children. I walked as in a daze, not knowing where I was going; but I stopped at City Hall and went into an office. When the woman at the desk asked how she could help me, I said, "I want help to buy a house." She didn't laugh at me; instead, she asked me to sit down. I did. She soon came back and asked me some questions; then she handed me a voucher for $14,000! This was incredible! But I wasn't dreaming. Perhaps the fact that I was nearly nine months pregnant had some bearing on the response I received.

Chapter 24

1960 – 1962: DISSOLUTION and REMARRIAGE

I was tired of going back to court when Randy did not adhere to the court obligations. My uncle, Rev. Hill helped me hire a lawyer. I began making plans to return to court after the baby's birth. The lawyer said it would be difficult for Randy to get a divorce because he had no grounds for one. But *I* could divorce *him*. That idea didn't sound right to me. I had promised to stay with Randy 'til death do us part', and I took my commitment seriously. So the lawyer came up with a term I could accept: dissolution.

Margaret Pauline Hooker was born December 14, 1960. When Margaret and I came home from the hospital, my doctor said I should go up and down the stairs only once per day. This really required organizational planning. Our bedrooms were on the second floor; the kitchen and living room were on the first floor. To access the apartment from the outside, it was necessary to climb a flight of stairs. My best ally was breast-feeding. I stayed on the first floor after dressing the children and sending Doug off to school. I bathed Margaret in the kitchen sink. For breakfast, I made biscuits so they could eat them throughout the day, if they became hungry between meals.

Randy reappeared. Our apartment was on his walking beat. He stopped by and brought Margaret downstairs every morning; in the afternoon, he stopped by to take her back upstairs. I was grateful that the children were getting a chance to see him again, but my mind was made up; he would not be allowed to live with us again. When he came by after the children's bedtime, I refused to let him in. David and Doug slept in a bedroom together. They had wrought iron twin beds, stacked one above the other. There was a ladder that could be used to reach the top bed. Doug was assigned the top bed because he was older; David still tossed in his sleep. One night, I was awakened from a sound sleep by a thud that seemed to shake the room. I heard nothing, but felt a need to check on the children. David sat dazed on the floor. He had climbed up into Doug's bed, and had tumbled out of bed onto the floor. The floors were concrete and we had no rugs to cover them. He had taken quite a fall. When I put him back to bed, he fell asleep.

But I didn't. My mind was racing about what I should do. As soon as the children woke up and had some breakfast, I put David in the stroller with Margaret and wheeled him down to St. Mary's hospital that was located about two blocks from our apartment. When I told the doctors in the emergency room what had happened, they refused to examine him. They asked why I had taken so long to bring him down. I explained that I could not leave the other children alone, so we came as soon as possible. Nevertheless, they would not examine him. If I had been able to think rationally I would have realized that David was not vomiting, and perhaps he was all right. But only a mother can understand my anxiety. The accident had happened late Saturday night; it was Sunday when I took him to the hospital.

I called the American Medical Association to tell them what had happened and asked them to recommend a doctor who might examine David. Their first question stunned me. "Do you have money to pay a doctor?" "Yes."

Fortunately, I had received $70.00 from Randy. When the AMA gave me a doctor's name, I had to take a taxi to the doctor's office. I left the children with Aunt Mildred. The taxi driver took David and me to a doctor whose office was attached to his home. When I explained what had happened to my child, the doctor asked, "Do you have money to pay for my service?"

I had to give him $20.00 before he examined David. After he X-rayed David's head, he told me that there was no fracture. "Watch him carefully for a while to see if he vomits or becomes sleepy unnecessarily." The trip to and from the doctor's office had depleted half of our allowance for two weeks. I was relieved that David was all right, but the incident further motivated me to take up my teaching career, so I could earn enough money to move from the projects.

The dissolution was final on April 5, 1961; the final judgment was that Randy was to send child support for the children and he was granted unstructured visitation.

As I planned our move out of the projects, I thought about some pleasant memorable experiences while living there. One of them involved Melanie. She did not demand a lot of attention, but she needed some, too. One time when I had been especially mean to her, my conscience convicted me. Before going to a PTA meeting, I decided to devote a whole block of time to Melanie. So I asked her if she wanted to help me make cookies. She was happy to do so. As I placed ingredients on a tray, I said, "Mommy will ask you to give me the ingredients, and you will hand them to me. O.K?" "All right, Mommy." I did not have an electric mixer; I had to hand-mix the dough. "All right, hand me the eggs." She handed them to me, one at a time. She had beautiful hands. "Now hand me the sugar." She did. In another bowl, I creamed the butter. "Now, hand me the flour." She was seated on the counter. She looked all around. Then she got up and turned around, still looking for the flour. I was busy stirring. After what seemed like a long time, I reached over, picked up the flour and added it to the other ingredients. From Melanie came this puzzled question. "Mommy, why is that called flour?"

It dawned on me that her perception of flour was the blossom. I tried to explain to her that this white powdery substance was also called flour. She had not learned to spell yet, so I couldn't expect her to distinguish between the two spellings. I explained, "This kind of flour is used in cooking; the other kind of flower grows in the garden." I saw a light bulb turn on inside her head. I realized that she had taught me an important lesson: children do not necessarily understand what adults mean when they speak. But if you pay attention to their facial expression, you can tell when they don't understand. And you can tell by the light in their eye when they learn something new.

After Margaret was born, I began making plans to find work as a teacher. This time when I went to the Board of Education, I was told that the only job I could have was teaching kindergarten. I accepted it. "But you can only teach kindergarten if you get a kindergarten certification." I was told.

I asked Mama to let my sister, Oreatha come to Cincinnati to take care of the children while I went back to school. My oldest brother, Anderson sent me money to pay for summer school. Mama sent me three dresses to wear. In June of 1961 I enrolled at the University of Cincinnati to obtain kindergarten certification. Every day, as I walked across the university campus, I talked with God. I asked Him to take care of Oreatha and my babies and to direct me as I planned life without Randy.

81

In the fall of 1961, I went to work for the Cincinnati Board of Education. As soon as I began receiving a monthly paycheck, my rent increased. I couldn't believe how much I was required to pay, but I was determined to save enough money to purchase a home for my family. Our first –and last- Christmas in the housing project was a pleasant one. With my first check from the Board of Education, I bought a pretty dress for Melanie. The children received some toys and some clothes that Christmas. As I watched them play with their new toys, I thanked God for His goodness to us. Nevertheless, I planned to move out of the public housing with all deliberate speed.

Meanwhile, my sister Pearline had begun working as a substitute teacher in the public schools. She was very successful, and was given a permanent position at an elementary school. One of the teachers she met at her new school was a real estate agent. That summer, Mrs. Douglas called me and offered to show me some houses. When I began to look at homes, I received a rude awakening: My $14,000 would hardly make a downpayment on a home, especially one that I wanted.

Mrs. Douglas thought that she had a possible solution. "Why don't you and Mr. Hooker reconcile? Then together you can afford a home for your children." Randy was open to this idea. Since the dissolution became final, he had worked overtime to re-enter our lives. The thought that I now had living wages because I was working and was receiving child support fueled his interest in remarrying. I wanted no part of it; I had had my fill of his cowardice. But as we looked at houses, it became more and more clear that it would take much longer for me to save the money alone. So, at Mrs. Douglas' suggestion, Randy was invited to house hunt with us. She would call and tell him where we would be looking that day. He met us at the house, and we looked at it together. However, I was adamant: I would not remarry him unless there was a home for our children.

The realtor took us to a street in a suburban neighborhood. One family on the street had sold their house to an African American family. Three more houses were for sale. White professionals owned them. We inspected them. They were all roomy and priced to sell. For the first time I witnessed the blessing of white flight. However, none of the homes seemed ideal to me. I needed a house that did not require immediate repairs. I wanted a back yard with grass so the children could play in safety.

Then the realtor said, "I have one more house to show you." We inspected it. It was a beautiful, well-kept three-floor Tudor home, set back from the street about 45 feet. There was a basketball hoop in the back yard. The back was terraced; grass was on the first terrace, shrubbery on the second, and on the third, there were many trees. I could picture the children playing outside in the grass. The boys could climb the trees. It was ideal. Looking back to the house from the driveway as the sun set, I said to Mrs. Douglas, "This is the one I want; I don't want to look at any more houses." Randy was unsure. "There is no way we can afford that house."

Mrs. Douglas took us for a visit to her employer, who tried to convince us that we could afford the house. However, the voucher I had received from city hall would not apply, because Randy and I were planning to buy the house together. We sat down with pencil and paper. I determined we could afford it; Randy was more reluctant.

Nevertheless, we began the process of purchasing the house. The Cincinnati Board of Education gave me a satisfactory rating and said I would be hired the next year. Randy got clearance from his work. Mr. Spencer found a lender. Meanwhile, we visited the house two more times. The owner agreed to our offer. The only thing needed at this point was our signature. Mrs. Douglas kept me apprised of the progress. The owner would be able to vacate the house in one month. There was one obstacle: Mr. Hooker would not agree to sign the final documents. My response to her was this: "If he does not sign, he can forget about remarriage. The children and I will make it on our own."

Her next communication was, "Mrs. Hooker, Mr. Hooker has agreed to sign. I will pick you up to go and see Mr. Spencer at 4:00 p.m." After we signed, reality set in. Neither of us had a savings account. We had no money for a down payment or closing costs.

I went back to God. "Lord, I know that this is no problem for You. If it is Your will for us to have that house, please arrange it. Thank you." On our next visit to Mr. Spencer's office, we were told everything had been arranged. Mr. Spencer obtained the required down payment for us. The owner would vacate the premises in 30 days, and we could take occupancy at that time. Again, I marveled at God's miracles!

After we closed on the house, Mr. Hooker became efficient. In a few days, he secured a marriage license and came to my apartment with the minister and a witness. I was making dinner when they arrived. I cleaned my hands, took off my apron, and we were remarried August 15, 1962. Then we began to make plans to move to our new home – together. We didn't have enough money to hire movers. My neighbor in the housing project helped Randy move our beds, clothing, a few toys, and kitchen utensils. Randy rented a U Haul truck. All our joint possessions fit easily in the truck.

On Thanksgiving Day, November 22, 1962 we moved into our first – and last home. I had strained my back while trying to move something, but Randy, Doug, Melanie, David, Margaret, and I had Thanksgiving dinner in the breakfast room of our new home!

After finishing my coursework at the University of Cincinnati in August of 1962, I had been certified to teach from Kindergarten through 12th grade. The Board of Education assigned me to teach kindergarten at two different schools: My morning class was taught downtown at Guilford Elementary School. I had a large, well-equipped, well-supplied classroom. There were 16 white pupils and one black pupil. In the afternoon, I went to Sands Elementary School in the West End. The classroom was unfurnished; no supplies were provided. I had 40 black pupils. My home school was Guilford, so for staff meetings it was necessary to return downtown. I left home at 6:00 a.m. and returned at 6:00 p.m. But that year was my most productive year as a teacher. The principal of the Guilford Elementary School, which was in a poor white Appalachian neighborhood, made home visitation mandatory. I set a goal to visit the home of every child in the afternoon Kindergarten as well. Children who came to school in the afternoon had gotten up early in the day. By the time they were to come to school, they were pretty worked up. I gave the parents the following suggestions: "Call your children in early for lunch. Allow them to calm down before sending them to school. Let then wash their hands for a long time; water play can be therapeutic. Then sit down and eat with them. Talk about what they can expect at school that day. Send them off with a hug and kiss." I'm convinced I was as helpful to the parents as I was to the children.

Randy owned a used car. It broke down, and without discussing it with me, he sold the car. I asked why. He said it would cost too much to repair it. Suddenly, I was back to using bus transportation again. I rode the bus in the morning to Guilford. At noon, I ate an apple on the bus on my way to Sands. On staff meeting days, usually Mondays, it was necessary to take a bus back downtown to Guilford. At the end of the day, I rode the bus home. Seldom, if ever, did the busses run on time. Standing in the wind, rain and snow waiting for them made for long days.

Child care for Margaret and her brothers and sister after school left much to be desired. We tried two or three different babysitters. One of them was a family member. She was very good, but due to some friction that I never really understood, she quit. Another woman watched television instead of watching Margaret. She left all the soiled dishes in the sink; she was just incompetent. Finally, in exasperation, I told Randy that we must find competent childcare or I could not work. Fortunately for us, there was a woman in the church who had lost her job as an elevator operator, because the hotel where she worked closed down. My Aunt Edna brought us together. At first, Mrs. Smith was apprehensive that she could please me, but she was willing to try. She proved to be a Godsend. She took care of our children for 17 years, missing 1/2 day for a funeral. I gladly paid her half my salary; when I got a raise, she got one, too. She arrived at the house at 7:30 every morning (Monday – Friday) and stayed until I got home from work. If I asked her, she would start dinner once in awhile. With her competence and loyalty, I was able to devote myself to my work, as I needed to. I was thankful that Mrs. Smith loved my children as her own, and they loved her. If there was an emergency at school, she returned my child; whatever was necessary, she did it.

In early February, we had a major snowstorm - seven inches of snow. Then the temperature dropped below zero. All the buses were running late. I felt like a Popsicle when I arrived at Guilford Elementary, and was surprised to find that only one of my pupils, Lila had come to school. The little girl was wearing a summer coat, had no hat, and no mittens. All she had on under her coat was a thin cotton dress, no socks, and a pair of wet tennis shoes.

At noon, I took the bus to Sands Elementary. The bus was so late, I thought I would freeze to death. I was surprised to see half of my afternoon pupils in the room, waiting eagerly for me to arrive. That warmed my heart.

For the rest of the month the weather was nasty. Lila was the only pupil to attend my morning class for the whole month of February. I discovered that the reason she came to school was because there was no heat in her mother's apartment. She told me that at night the whole family slept in one bed to keep warm. She came to class to thaw out. With me as her personal tutor, she flourished, making great progress in reading and math.

When my supervisor visited my classes in late April, she was particularly pleased to see the progress made by the afternoon class. All 40 pupils were attentive and well disciplined. When I sat down to play the piano, instantly the children gathered around it and began to sing along. She complimented me on the way I incorporated music as a means of instruction, and invited me to participate as a leader at the next teacher training seminar.

On her recommendation, the next year I was assigned to Washington Elementary School, located in a predominantly white Appalachian community. The grade I was to teach was called pre-first. The parents in this neighborhood were reluctant to send their children to school until the law dictated they must at age six. Consequently, these children had no preschool or kindergarten experiences. They were old enough to be in first grade, but lacked kindergarten skills. My challenge was to prepare them for first grade. My supervisor told me I could not use the kindergarten curriculum materials or the first grade curriculum. So I wrote my own. When eight of my 23 pupils tested into the second grade, I was asked to share my curriculum. I refused. For the remainder of my time at the school, the second grade teachers began requesting some of my pupils.

Over the strong objections of my principal, I visited the homes of every one of my pupils. The parents did not always invite me in. On more than one occasion, I had to talk with the parent from the street or the alley through an open window. On these visits, I made it clear that I had an open door policy: parents were welcomed to come visit the classroom any time they chose. And they came. Two of these parents stand out in my mind. Mrs. Ford was an older mother of two young boys. Her husband had died. They had older adult children, but she had the responsibility of rearing these two young boys by herself. She came and sat in the classroom every day at math time. She would sit right behind the children in the group. I could tell by the expression on her face that our activities fascinated her.

For example, to teach the children how to write numerals, I used aluminum pie pans with sand. As we wrote the numeral, we sang: A line straight down and a line straight down, A line straight down and a line straight down, A line straight down and a line straight down, and that is Mr. One. For two: Around and down and add a line, Around and down and add a line, Around and down and add a line, And that is Mr. Two. For three: Half around and half around, Half around and half around, Half around and half around, and that is Mr. Three. Each time we wrote a numeral, we would shake the sand, smoothing it for the next numeral. This tactile approach helped the children learn to write the numerals before writing them on paper. Learning was fun in our class; the children responded enthusiastically. The high attendance confirmed that they liked to come to school.

Years after I retired, I met Mrs. Ford at a local grocery store where she was working. She said to me candidly. "You know, I learned place value when you taught it to John and his classmates." Remarks like this are the invaluable reward teachers receive for their labors.

I observed that one little girl, Judy had what I thought was a hearing problem. I invited her mother to visit with me after school. I shared my suspicions. She said that she suspected that her daughter had a hearing loss, but the family's financial means did not provide the resources to do anything about it. I encouraged her to get help for her daughter, saying, "If I were you, I would not consider the cost; I would get a good diagnosis and go from there."

She took her daughter for a medical assessment, and discovered that the child's condition was not reversible, but the hearing loss could be retarded. She was so appreciative of my concern, she came to class to observe. She became a regular volunteer in my classroom She watched me as I made sure Judy was looking at me before I spoke to her. My speech was slow and deliberate. To be sure Judy understood what I had said, I would ask her to repeat the words to me. After I was assured she understood what I meant, I would leave her and work with other children. The mother began to use these techniques with Judy at home, and she became a volunteer teacher's assistant in the classroom.

At the end of the year, I went to the principal to recommend that Judy be allowed to skip first grade and be promoted to second grade. I took some of Judy's papers along so I could document the quality of her work. I was nervous and the papers were shaking in my hand. He took the papers out of my hand, saying, "I know she's ready for second grade. Go ahead and promote her."

The principal soon also discovered Judy's mother's ability. She was asked to be a volunteer in the school library. The next year the School Board hired her to be a central office librarian. In spite of her hearing impairment, Judy graduated from high school and enrolled in a secretarial training program. She became an excellent secretary and she earned a good living. From time to time when I met them in the community, the mother was grateful for my encouragement.

Chapter 25

1962 – 1968: FAMILY LIFE

My own children were growing and getting involved in after school activities. With a new car, I became the parent who did most of the chauffeuring and accommodating their participation in extra activities. When Doug was in third grade, he came home one day with a request to learn to play the violin. From my thirty-five dollar grocery allotment, I paid three dollars for weekly lessons and three dollars toward the purchase of a violin. I took him to lessons and attended most of his concerts.

Melanie said, "Mommy may I take art lessons?" I knew that one of our neighbors was teaching art lessons to children in the neighborhood, so I agreed to take Melanie there once a week. Another neighbor was teaching dance to the neighborhood children. She asked if she could use our basement. Margaret and Melanie joined her class.

David asked if he could join a Little League baseball team. The team practiced in a nearby park. So I drove him to practice five days a week.

I wanted our sons to be exposed to scouting, so I organized a community scout troop. I recruited a neighbor to become scoutmaster; he had three sons, so this worked well. Of course, I had to be a den mother. David observed these activities with his older brother, and anticipated being a Cub Scout when he reached the required age. One day he said to me, "Mommy, will you be my den mother when I am old enough to be a scout?" I said, "Of course I will"

Once a week, about eight boys gathered at my house. Sometimes, they arrived at my house before I got home from work. The neighbors complained that the boys cut across their lawns. One of the first lessons they had to learn was that Cub Scouts are respectful of other people's property; they are helpful and not destructive.

One of the activities the boys enjoyed took place at the District Camp. Our task was to set up an Indian teepee. We assembled it in my back yard, then folded it to take to the Camporee. At our Halloween party, I had planned to have the boys bob for apples. But the weather was cold and I didn't want to send them home wet, so I hung the apples from a clothesline. I tied their hands behind their backs. The challenge was to bite the apple without using their hands.

I enjoyed the time spent with my children during summer breaks. It was difficult finding meaningful chores for them. Then there was the challenge to make sure they performed their chores without my nagging them. During the school year, Mrs. Smith took care of a number of chores that would ordinarily fall to them, and they were reluctant to accept responsibility when she was absent.

Most of their chores were confined to the inside of the house: making their beds, picking up after themselves, washing dishes, and taking out garbage. I posted charts in the kitchen and in the bathroom outlining tasks, with stars as rewards for completing chores without being reminded. I wanted to enjoy the summers with them, not be the taskmaster. Surprisingly they cooperated.

One of my nephews, Murray, Jr. had a serious accident with a power lawn mower the summer of 1967. He reached under a lawnmower before turning off the motor, and cut two fingers on his right hand. That was a traumatic time for all. He had been learning to play the clarinet. Although the adults grieved his loss, he took it in stride. There were several surgeries on his hand, but one finger was lost permanently. The next year, he began writing with his left hand, and switched from playing the clarinet to playing the drums. Coping with his accident prompted him to become a medical doctor.

The next summer the dishwasher broke down. I took the occasion to teach my children how to wash dishes. Their dad always prompted them to say thank you at meals. Then I would ask, "Who wants to do the dishes?" No one volunteered. So, I began assigning the task. Doug, Melanie, and David all took turns. But Margaret was too young to wash dishes alone, so I let her help me. They asked, "Mommy, when are you going to get the dishwasher fixed?" I decided we didn't need to repair the dishwasher, saying, "Grandmama Pauline would be surprised to learn that you don't know how to wash dishes." Eventually, we discarded the broken dishwasher; I never replaced it.

After their morning chores, the children always enjoyed playing outside. After breakfast, they explored in the woods. They discovered all kinds of things, including a drainage ditch. They enjoyed playing in the ditch and came home muddy. After Randy investigated, we ordered them not to play there anymore.

On another occasion, David was playing detective. One day he burst into the house exclaiming, "Dad, I think some man has been spying on us!" "Why do you think so, David?" "There're some cigarette butts on the ground; beside a log in the woods, overlooking our house. Come on! I'll show you." The two went up to investigate. Indeed, there were cigarette butts on the ground. David's dad, the policeman took care of the matter.

When David was four and Doug was nine, they often played Robin Hood in the woods. Doug had asked his dad for a bow and arrows. Dad said "No," so Doug made his own. One day, just as I was about to call the children in for lunch, I heard a bloodcurdling scream. David was on the ground howling; Doug stood over him in shock. With his homemade bow and stick arrow, he had shot his brother in the eye. Our neighbor across the street had just finished eating lunch and was about to return to work. I ran around the house, carrying David in my arms. The neighbor looked to see what the commotion was about. I yelled to him, "Mr. Noble, will you take me to the hospital? David has been shot in the eye with a stick!"

In my rush to get David to the hospital I forgot about the other children. The examination revealed that the stick had indeed struck David in the eye. When I got my bearings, I called Randy at work. Immediately, he arrived at the hospital. The doctors explained that David would have to be kept quiet for a few days, and he would have to remain in the hospital. After he was sedated and put to bed for the night, Randy and I returned home to see about the other children. At dinner, we explained to them that David would have to remain at the hospital for a few days. "Can we go to see him?" Dad said, "No, David has to remain quiet."

Suddenly, Doug broke forth crying inconsolably. In our concern for David, neither of us had realized what Doug must have been going through after accidentally shooting his brother in the eye. His dad and I hugged and comforted him. "Of course we know you are sorry. We know you would never hurt your little brother on purpose." The Hooker household was somber that evening.

Randy and I took turns visiting David in the hospital. To keep him immobile, it was necessary to tie one leg in traction. His eye was bandaged: he was quite helpless, yet his spirits were as high as ever. He enjoyed the attention paid to him, but he wanted to go home to play with his siblings. He spent at least a week in the hospital. It was difficult to keep him quiet. Thank God, he suffered no permanent damage to the eye. The children were subdued until he came home. They were so happy to see him – as happy as he was to see them. That would be the last summer I spent with them free of other responsibilities.

In 1964 I decided to go back to the university and earn a master's degree in Education Administration. For the next four years I took courses –summer and winter while working full-time and caring for my family. I really felt that I should prepare myself in case it ever became necessary for me to support my children and myself. Shortly, Margaret would be going to school full time; now was my time to advance in my career.

During that same summer, some of the primary teachers were offered the opportunity to take a two week intensive course in Indianapolis; the goal was to prepare to teach Head Start. We would receive credits and get paid. I took advantage of the offer. We enrolled Melanie, David, and Margaret in a day camp during my absence. Doug stayed with his cousins. Randy was left in charge of the children. At the end of the two weeks, he called and said he was coming to meet me at school and drive me home.

I was delighted! He arrived on campus the evening before the last day. He went with me to class the next day. On my way to class for the last time, some of the women were teasing us, saying that my husband couldn't be separated from his wife for two weeks. On the way home I was chatty and excited about seeing the children again.

Then he broke the news. "Dess, I want you to be prepared when you see David. He had a fall on the monkey bars at school and got banged up pretty badly." My heart skipped a beat. I could hardly wait to see him.

In spite of Randy's warning, when I first saw David, I was shocked! His head was swollen twice its normal size. His face was black and blue. He whimpered when I touched his face. But he was so happy to see me! The other children surely felt neglected as I picked him up and hugged him. "What happened to you?" "I fell on the monkey bars."

Randy explained that David had climbed to the top of the bars and fell off. Over the next few days I tried to get a more detailed account of what had happened. The daycare provider said something about somebody polishing the monkey bars; David didn't grip them tightly, and slipped.

I was ready to sue her. Her husband was a policeman, so Randy opposed that idea. David received medical attention; he was all right. I blamed myself for leaving them. This hurt Randy's feelings; he said I didn't think anyone else could care for the children properly. At that moment I was in no mood for his self-pity; someone had been negligent, and our son was hurt. But David healed all right. And he survived the summer at a different day care center.

For the rest of the summer I taught Head Start. Margaret went with me to school everyday. She loved it. She was the principal's pet. One of my Head Start students was so sad because he had to move. "Mrs. Hooker, will you take my dog and keep him?" Keith asked me. I was caught off guard. His eyes were pleading. "Of course, I'll keep your dog, Keith."

Randy and I picked Sport up one Saturday morning. He was a handsome dog: a mixture of Collie and Dachshund. He had long golden hair and stood about 10 inches high. He had a doghouse made from a barrel. He and David bonded instantly; they were inseparable. But Sport did not want to stay outside; he wanted to be with David. Randy reluctantly allowed him to remain in the house. At meal times, he curled up under the table where David sat. David "accidentally" dropped food. After dinner Sport could stay in the room with them until it was time for David to go to bed. Randy would tell David to take Sport to the basement. Sport would crawl under the bed and lock his feet in the bedsprings. David could not dislodge him. But as soon as Randy called him, Sport would come out with his tail between his legs and whine as he was led to the basement.

Sport's bark was very gruff. He was confined to the house during the day, but as soon as I got home, I let him out to run for about 20 minutes. He would come back and sit at the edge of the walkway in front of the house. He guarded our house, the house next door, and the one across the street. He was not attracted to passing cars, but if someone passed on a bicycle, he would chase him. One day a little girl came by on her bike. Sport chased her; she fell and skinned her knee. Her mother came to our door and angrily announced that she was going to sue me.

My remarks were directed to the little girl. "Come in and let me clean your knee." I washed it and applied first-aid cream and a Band-Aid. As I cleaned her knee I talked to her. "Sport didn't mean to scare you. He likes children. But his way of talking is to bark. He just wanted to play with you. Come here Sport and speak to this little girl. Tell her you are sorry. See! He likes you. Touch him."

This took the sting our of mother's bark. But I had to teach Sport not to run after bicycles. We would sit on the porch together. I wrapped gauze around his mouth. When a bicycle rider came by, I said, "No, Sport" He would whine, but after a few days he learned not to chase passing bicycle riders.

In the fall, I returned to teaching pre-first grade pupils at Washington Elementary. At the same time I continued graduate studies at the University of Cincinnati. We still had only one car, so I attended classes at the university by riding the bus.

Dean Good was my education research professor. When I looked at the bus schedule I saw that one bus would get me to school more than thirty minutes too early. The next one would arrive five minutes late. I decided I would take the second bus, rather than wasting my time sitting in an empty classroom. Every week when I arrived, Dean Good made a sarcastic remark about people who are late to class. He never said anything to me directly, but he wanted to make me uncomfortable. He didn't succeed. I ignored him as I had ignored my sixth grade teacher. I pretended I didn't know what he was talking about. If he had spoken to me directly, I would have explained to him that I was doing my best. I had four children at home, and I needed every possible minute with them before I left for class. This wasn't an excuse; it was a fact. This white professor made it a regular habit to announce that he didn't think African Americans were capable of earning a grade higher than a C. I fulfilled the requirements of the course. He gave me a C – the only grade I received lower than a B as a graduate student.

One of my classmates, Essie Jackson, decided not to let Dean Good know that she was black. She decided that since the class was so large, she would sit in the back of the room and keep her mouth shut. All of her assignments were returned with a letter grade of A, and she got A on her finals. She picked up her final exam after the course was over; then she went to his office and introduced herself. Dean Good's face turned red. Essie exposed Dean Good's bigotry.

The summer before I graduated, Randy took the children to visit our parents so I could study without interruptions. Sport stayed at my heels when I came home each day from the university. At night, he slept across the doorway of our bedroom. He understood that he was not allowed in our bedroom, and he was obedient even though Randy was not at home. One night, I heard him go downstairs. He didn't ask to go outside, so I stayed in bed. The next morning I went into the kitchen and found a dead bat. I had left dishwater in the sink, and it had drowned. Sport had heard the bat and had gone downstairs to investigate. This to me was another sign of God's grace. Ordinarily, I never left dishwater in the sink. The bat had entered the house through the kitchen exhaust fan. I was so thankful for Sport's care of me. I shared this with the children when they came home. They too had some exciting news to share with me.

Doug had contracted athlete's foot; Randy ignored it. When they got home, Doug's foot was raw. He had to be taken to the doctor. It seemed every time Randy cared for the children something bad happened.

By the end of the summer I was tired of school; I decided to have my diploma mailed to me. Randy said, "You must let the children see you march. You have sacrificed all this time to complete the work; they deserve to see you march."

However, the morning of graduation, Randy announced that Sport would have to go. Earlier that summer our next door neighbor had found a Beagle puppy. She penned the dog up at the top of the hill.

95

He got away. Now she accused my children of letting him out. She also complained when Sport ran across her yard each day. Randy was summoned to court. The judge reprimanded and fined him $100. Randy's decision was final. Sport had to go!

That announcement spoiled my graduation. I marched across the stage with a heavy heart. Still, the children were proud of me. I believe that is why all of them struggled to earn their college degrees; I want to believe that I modeled for them my high expectations.

When I arrived home, Sport and I went up in the woods. I cried as I explained to him that he had to leave us. He seemed to understand. He too was sad.

My first thought was to try to contact Keith, Sport's former owner. When I called the number, Keith's dad answered. He was so happy to know that I wanted them to take Sport back. He said. "You know, Mrs. Hooker as soon as we arrived at this new place, we saw people with dogs. Keith wanted to call you and take Sport back then, but I told him that would be unfair. Your family had been kind enough to take Sport, and it would be unfair for us to take him back. But now I'll be there in 20 minutes."

He was. And Sport ran and jumped into his arms! He remembered his former master. He was a very intelligent dog. David grieved his loss, but soon accepted that Sport had been a good friend for a while but had to return home.

Later that year our neighbor had an opportunity to confess that she regretted forcing us to give Sport up. She called me one night; her voice sounded frightened. She whispered into the telephone, "I'm in my bedroom upstairs; someone has broken into the house! Please call the police!"

I called the police. If Sport had been at home, she would have received protection from the intruder. By way of apology, she made the same observation. But Sport was happy to be back with his original family. And we were happy for him.

With Margaret ready to enter first grade, and with my degree in Education Administration and Supervision in hand, I thought I was now ready to advance my career.

I left Washington Elementary because I got pregnant in my fifth year. The staff gave me a big going away baby shower and reception. They gave me so many clothes and furnishings for the baby, that it was not necessary to buy clothing for him for nearly two years. The principal called me into his office after the party saying, "In my time here at Washington Elementary, I have never seen the kind of parental involvement you have had in your classes. Tell me your secret."

I responded, "Hire a black teacher. When word gets out, parents will be curious. Many mothers came to see if their child had that new "black teacher." When they came, I found out if they were creative and I made it a point to find ways to involve them in the class work. For example, I knew that Mrs. Ford, the older mother with the two young boys, had a woodworking shop in her basement. She told me that she learned how to use the tools while her husband was still alive. She enjoyed woodworking, and she wanted to help the children make Christmas gifts for their parents. One day she came to class with a note holder she had made. She had cut out a square, 4-inch base, drilled a hole in the center, glued a dowel in the hole, cut a diagonal slant at the top of the dowel and glued a clothespin to the top. Last, It was spray painted green. She had also found a poem addressed to both parents, stating how the tool could be used as a recipe holder or a letter holder. Her idea was to prepare the parts and have the children assemble and paint them. I gave her permission to work with two or three of the children at a time. She took them unobtrusively from the classroom and soon returned with them to get two or three more. The children were proud of what they had made, and delighted to have a Christmas gift to give to their parents.

The supervisor also took note of my skills. I was asked to help write a curriculum titled "Teaching Reading Through Music".

Chapter 26

1969 – 1970: FIFTH CHILD and SECOND DIVORCE

Randy seemed resentful of my pregnancy and from that time on he refused to partake in regular family activities. When the school staff gave me the baby shower, he refused to attend to help me take the gifts home. He wanted to have nothing to do with planning for a new baby. I took advantage of the circumstances to teach the children about what to expect when a new baby comes into the family. The children were asked to find a name for the baby. I told them to choose a boy's name beginning with the letter "D." I explained, "In our family, all the boys' names begin with D as in daddy and all the girls' names begin with M as in mother." After each visit to the doctor, I shared with them my pregnancy progress. They enthusiastically engaged in the naming of the baby. One day two of them came home with the same proposal: the baby should be named Damon.

Margaret said, "Please don't name him Damon because Damon is a demon. One of my classmates is named Damon and he teases me a lot." A few days later, they decided upon the name Darrell. I decided to spell his name D-a-r- r-e-l-l because I had experienced that some first graders had difficulty learning to write the letter "y" with the tail placed below the line.

The baby was due to arrive at the end of August 1969. Fortunately, the curriculum writing was completed before the doctor told me I had to stop driving. This order caused a small problem. With the limitation of my activities, the children were also limited. They had to stay near the house because I might need them when the baby arrived. To keep the children occupied. I gave each of them their accumulated school photographs. They were also given a large piece of Bristol board, magazines, scissors, and glue. I challenged them to use the supplies to create a poster that showed their individual personality. They worked at this project for hours. They posted their finished products on their bedroom walls and my bedroom wall, and anywhere else they could find a space.

We didn't have a television set. Usually the children enjoyed playing outside in the summer, but now they were constrained to stay close to home. Most of their activities came to a halt. I appreciated their help. When possible, Randy was recruited to participate in their activities. He was surprised to witness some of the things they were doing. For example, one Sunday he accompanied Doug to a concert. Randy came home and said to me, "You know, Dess, I looked at Doug and marveled at how well he performed. He is a fine young man and I realize I have had very little input into his rearing." He meant it as a compliment to me, but I hoped he realized he needed to be more involved in their lives.

Another Sunday in August Randy took the children to church. While they were gone, I made a birthday cake for Randy – his birthday is August tenth. It was necessary to use the ingredients I had on hand because I couldn't drive to the store. I congratulated myself on producing what I thought was a good creation. I took confectioner's sugar and butter and made cream frosting. I took chocolate and wrote "Happy Birthday, Daddy." Randy was unimpressed. The children thought it looked pretty.

David had a little league game that afternoon, so Randy took him to play. When they came home I quizzed David about the game. He was so happy to have had his daddy watch him play. But Randy lambasted him for being so stupid. I stared at him, but kept my mouth shut. David might have made mistakes, but he was only 10 years old! I could not hold my anger in. "How could you do that to your young son? After all, you haven't taken time to teach him any skills, although you are quite capable. You went to college on an athletic scholarship, but you haven't even played catch with your sons!" I had dinner waiting, so we began to eat. Randy couldn't stop. David was showing his sadness at disappointing his daddy. Everyone was quiet as Randy ranted. Finally I said, "Stop it! How can you do this to him? He was only trying to impress you." When Randy continued, I threw water in his face. He jumped up and threw water back at me. The children began to cry and come to my defense. The next door neighbor heard the ruckus and came over to investigate. Randy stormed out the door. I assured her we were fine.

I don't know when Randy came back that night. After he left, I helped the children regain composure. We cleaned the kitchen and retired to bed. From that day forward, things began to deteriorate further.

I was determined to keep my composure. It was unfair to the children to witness their daddy and mother fighting. However, they retreated further into themselves; they only relaxed when their daddy was away from home. The strain continued.

To add to Randy's dilemma, he learned that one of his brothers had been diagnosed with a brain tumor. Randy was torn between attending to our family needs and going to see his brother. The baby's imminent birth won out, but the strain continued for Randy. The fact that Darrell's arrival was overdue didn't help the situation.

I began to experience labor that would last four hours maximum, then stop. The doctor's mother was ill; she lived out of the country. Dr. Bassette traveled back and forth to check on his mother. His patients were assigned to another doctor.

About two weeks after Darrell's due arrival, I went into labor again. I called the doctor who was substituting for Dr. Bassette He asked how close the pains were, and suggested I call him back when they were closer together. Suddenly, as in the past, the pains stopped. There was no movement from the baby for the next few hours. I was beginning to be very concerned.

When Dr. Bassette came back the next week I called and reported to him what had been happening. On September 9th he ordered me to come to the hospital. He tried inducing labor. And it happened again. After four hours, movement stopped. Dr. Bassette tried to sound confident. "This isn't the first time your baby has come late, so we'll wait."

September had arrived; school was to start the next week. Melanie would be entering high school and she was nervous about the new environment.

On September 16, 1969, the "water" broke. This time it was the real thing for sure; the baby was long overdue. The nurses prepared me for the delivery. I reminded them that I did not want a sedative. When Dr. Bassette arrived and examined me, I heard him issue a terse order: "Prepare her for surgery!"

"What is wrong, Dr. Bassette?" "It's all right, Mrs. Hooker. We are going to have to take the baby." I stiffened with anxiety. What was happening? The preparation proceeded rapidly. They gave me a spinal anesthetic so I could be awake during the operation. Dr. Bassette talked with me as he worked. "Who is this one, Mrs. Hooker?" The pain medicine effectively blunted the pain, but I could feel the sensation of the knife as he opened my stomach. Momentarily, I heard Darrell cry. "Let me see him! Let me see him!" I demanded. Dr. Bassette calmly responded, "Let us clean him up first, Mrs. Hooker. Then you and Mr. Hooker can see him at the same time." He was beautiful! And big! There was the distinct coloring that looked like sideburns. Of course he was asleep. As we looked at him, I said to Randy, "Isn't he beautiful!" Later, in my room, I tried to talk with Randy about our new son. "What should we name him?" "I don't know, Dess. Didn't you and the children already choose a name for him?" "But what do you want to name him?" "I don't care."

I was so disappointed and hurt. Randy was still angry about this new addition to our family. I turned my back and went to sleep.

The next day, I remembered the other children. I asked for a telephone and I called home to ask Mrs. Smith how they were doing. She said Melanie was nervous about her first day at Walnut Hills. The other children were eagerly waiting to see their new brother. I placed a call to Walnut Hills and spoke to a freshmen counselor. I explained to him my concern about Melanie and asked him to tell her that her mother and the new baby were doing fine. She told me later that she was summoned to the counselor's office. He assured her that Darrell Walker Hooker and I were doing fine. She said she was so impressed by being singled out to go to the counselor's office, especially when she was told good news.

The Board of Education had granted me a leave of absence for maternity, and I was expected to return to work shortly after the school year began. But I couldn't do that to my baby. His brothers and sisters had been breast-fed; he deserved the same opportunity. I wanted a longer leave; when the Board denied my request, I resigned my job.

Randy did not take that news well. He began to withdraw from the family. He refused to pay the bills. He stayed away from home. The situation became tense. Despite efforts to get him to discuss his feeling, he refused to communicate. Meanwhile, Randy took a job as a supervisor at Seagram's Distillery in Lawrenceburg, Indiana. But he would not share with me any information about what was going on in his mind. Gradually, calls came in about overdue bills. The children were showing the effects of the strain in their grades. Margaret's math teacher requested a conference.

David began to act out in class. I knew the one way I could get help was to pray. And I did. More and more the children seemed to be unaware of their daddy's strange behavior; for that I was thankful. But the bill collectors were calling more frequently. I reported the calls to Randy; he remained silent.

Then, in July 1970, he stayed away from home for the July 4th celebration. A family from his new workplace came by to visit. They stayed all day, but Randy did not appear. In August 1970, he moved out again.

I was relieved in a way. The tension abated, and although I didn't know what we would do financially, I felt relieved that we no longer had to experience Randy's erratic negative behavior.

Darrell was less than a year old; I had no job. So, I turned to God for guidance and help. My neighbors were magnificent! One neighbor sent me $75.00; the instructions were to buy food for the children. A neighbor who lived next door came by frequently and looked in the refrigerator to see for herself whether we needed food. Their warm and caring help was much appreciated, but I knew I had to get a job.

As usual, when I needed guidance, I prayed. One day I was prompted to withdraw my retirement savings. With the money, I first purchased an annuity with the American Bible Society; that was my tithe and thank you for God's guidance. Then I paid off the balance on my car. The remaining funds provided us living expenses for a while.

The children had not been given anything for Christmas, so we went shopping. Each of them was allowed to choose one item of clothing for purchase.

I tried working as an encyclopedia salesperson for the summer because the flexibility allowed me to be at home with the children and take care of the baby. One day, I was changing Darrell's diaper. He was on his dressing table but he was not strapped in. Suddenly the telephone rang, It was my sales supervisor. While my back was turned the baby fell to the floor! I knew then that having this job would not work. Meanwhile, the courts had ordered Randy to send us child support money; again he sent what he wanted, when he wanted.

Chapter 27

1970: MIRACLES of MIRACLES

Circumstances came to a head over the Labor Day Weekend. Randy had traveled to California for work. He sent us a money order for child support. It was less than the amount he owed, but I welcomed it anyway. I had decided to seek out Legal Aid and get help. I also wanted to look for a job. Mrs. Smith was asked to come and stay with the baby while I ran some errands.

My first stop was the bank to cash the money order. The bank teller would not cash it; it was from out-of-town, so I would need to wait one week for clearance. Next, I went to Legal Aid. I arrived there at 10:00a.m. but didn't have an appointment; so I waited until 2:00 p.m. only to be told that they could not help me because my husband earned too much money. "That's why I'm here- to get my fair share of it." "Sorry, we can't help you."

I went into the restroom and cried out to God. "Lord, what do you want me to do! You know I have no money. The bank refused to cash the money order Randy sent us. I can't even pay Mrs. Smith for her help today. What should I do?" A distinct voice said to me, "Go to the Board of Education." "But Lord! I resigned my job with the Board of Education. School has been in session for a week already. Anyway, I don't have enough gasoline to get there!" "Go to the board of education!" "Yes, Lord, if You say so."

I washed my face, got in the car and drove to the Board of Education. I didn't even have enough money to feed a parking meter, but by now I was confident of Who was in charge. When I pulled up to the front of the Board of Education building, another car pulled out, and I took that spot. I glanced at the meter: Twenty minutes. Taking an elevator, I went to the tenth floor. As I signed in, I noticed that the room was full of people. There was no way I could get out of there before the meter expired! But before I could begin reading a magazine, my name was called. I was ushered onto the office of the Director of Personnel.

"Mrs. Hooker, you have a choice of two schools: Roll Hill or North Avondale." North Avondale was right around the corner from my

104

house! "I'll take North Avondale, thank you." I signed the papers and got up to leave. The Director said, "Mrs. Hooker, if you had waited three more days your tenure would have expired." "Thank You, Lord!"

As I walked back to my car, I thought, "God intended that I go to the Board of Education. He knew that my tenure was about to expire. He knew that the principal at North Avondale had called the Board and reported that she had to replace a teacher immediately. And He had reserved that job for me. So, He deliberately blocked all my efforts and steered me to the Board of Education." I marvel at God's grace!

To avoid running out of gasoline on the expressway, I decided to return home via Vine Street; then, if the car ran out of gas, it would be closer to home. Another miracle: it didn't run out of gas! And, just as I reached the corner of McMillan and Vine, God said, "Go back to the bank!" "But Lord!" "Go back to the bank!" "Yes, Lord." When I pulled up to the window, He said, "Cash in the baby's savings account." I had completely forgotten about it. When Darrell was born, Aunt Edna had opened a bank account for him. I had added to it $2.00 weekly. I found the savings book at the bottom of my purse.

The Teller remembered me, and immediately assumed that I returned to try to cash the money order again. "I'm sorry, Mrs. Hooker. I hope you understand that our policy…" I interrupted her. "Please close this account." I shoved the saving's book in the window. "I was only following - " Again I interrupted, "Are you going to tell me I can't cash in this account?" "No. Of course you can." "Thank you."

I took the money, went across the street to buy gas, and then went to North Avondale School. The Director of personnel had told me to stop by and let the principal know that I would be starting on Monday. The principal did not seem surprised to see me. She greeted me warmly and introduced me to the teacher I would be replacing. As the teacher and I walked across the campus to the classroom, she explained her philosophy of teaching. She believed in letting the children do what they wanted and they would learn in a relaxed atmosphere.

When I stepped into the classroom, my jaw dropped. She had indeed allowed the children to do whatever they wanted. Paint was on the floor, the ceiling and on tables and chairs! I thought "What was she thinking?" This was no atmosphere for learning.

I told the principal that I wanted to clean the room the next day, Saturday, because there was no way I could work in that room before it was cleaned. She said, "Odessa, it is a violation of Board policy to allow teachers in the buildings on off days without special permission."

"I'm sorry, Dr. O'Donnell, but I can't work in that room as it is." I begged, "Please call the Board and get permission for me to come tomorrow and clean up this mess."

She called and permission was granted. I went home to announce to Mrs. Smith that she would officially be starting with us again on Monday. Meanwhile, her services were needed the next day so I could clean the classroom. On Saturday I took a pail, brushes and cleaning supplies and cleaned that room. Then I went to the beauty parlor for the first time since Darrell was born (I would not take my baby into a beauty parlor with its smoke and polluted air). After the visit to the beauty parlor I felt presentable and alive again. The words from Ephesians 3:20 echoed in my mind. "[He] is able to do immeasurably more than all we ask or imagine, according to His power that is at work within us."

Chapter 28

1971: MORE DIVINE BLESSINGS and COUNSEL

To accommodate my need for help with Darrell in the afternoon, I assigned each of his brothers and sisters to care for him after school. They were completely responsible for his care; they had to supervise him, change his diapers, and whatever else needed to be done until I finished dinner. I fed him dinner, bathed him, and tucked him into bed each night. Doug was assigned Mondays, Margaret, Tuesdays, David, Wednesdays and Melanie Thursdays. I took over on weekends. Doug and Margaret were very good with him. On Wednesdays, Darrell would whimper, and on Thursdays he was very fretful. David teased him on Wednesdays; sometimes he tolerated it, sometimes he was aggravated. He cried practically all afternoon on Thursdays. I suggested to Melanie that she take him for a walk in his stroller. She said, "I'm not taking him for a walk. People will think that's my baby." I was surprised at her comment. She was only thirteen years old; anyway, everybody on the street knew that Darrell was my baby.

Nevertheless, she would not take him outside. He had to endure her care; I refused to rescue her or him. I faced other challenges. One was purchasing clothes to wear to work. I had not worked regularly for more than a year; I really needed more clothes.

One evening, the next door neighbor, Estelle Berman and I went to a neighborhood meeting. On the way home, as I was getting out of the car, she said, "You are a professional working woman. You need more clothes." "I know, but right now the children need clothes, too. And, because they are growing, their needs can't wait." "Would you allow me to give you some of my clothes?" "Of course. Thank you."

We wore the same size clothing. For the next 10 –12 years she gave me clothes four times per year: summer, spring, fall and winter. Furthermore, I was one of the best-dressed teachers at school. I only had to buy shoes and lingerie. God was still blessing me.

That solved the problem of new clothes, but there was an even greater problem. Randy had not paid the mortgage for three months.

The bank was threatening us with foreclosure. My neighbors, Dr. and Mrs. Berman came to the rescue again. They loaned me the money to satisfy the creditors. After a few months, we were in the black again. But other creditors called. Some of them were so nasty. I explained to them that my husband had made those purchases, and I would not pay them. "But you signed for them, too." "I did not." "Well some woman signed. You'd better find out who she was." "No, you find out who she was. And, if you continue to badger me, I will see a lawyer."

They resorted to some of the nastiest tactics I have ever witnessed. They sent notices to my work site without a name; that required the secretary to open them to determine to whom they were addressed. Fortunately, the secretary and the principal knew what was happening, so they helped me as much as they could. I was allowed time off to go to court several times, and they covered for me so my classes did not require a substitute teacher.

I filed a complaint against Randy for not sending the child support money. When the case came up for a hearing, the judge gave Randy a slap on the wrist and added the arrearage to the existing overdue balance. And, of course, he didn't pay it. This continued until one day I said to my lawyer, "I want to request a wage assignment." He stared back at me in surprise. "Wage assignment? You know, some employers won't agree to a wage assignment." "Call right now. Let's find out." He called. The employer was happy to comply. Now, the child support money would be taken out up front; what was left over would go to Randy.

Randy became very interested in us again now that we were getting our child support money. He often called to ask about the children's welfare. He even suggested that we really needed to be together to rear the children. I agreed with his logic, but I refused to live with him again. Once he called and asked me to go to dinner with him. He took me to the airport. I must admit the scenery was beautiful, and it felt like a real treat. But, as we were driving home, we go stuck in a major traffic jam. I took advantage of the opportunity.

"You know I have been talking to God about your coming to the house whenever you feel like it. It upsets the children and me. I have petitioned the courts twice about restricting your visitations. Each time the judge has said 'He can go and come as he pleases. He pays the bills.' But then I was talking to God. He said: 'When Noah built the ark, who kept the key?' 'Lord, I'm not talking about Noah. What should I do about Randy?' 'When Noah built the ark, who kept the key?' 'You did, Lord.' 'Well, I have the key; Randy won't come back to live in the house unless I let him.' ... So unless there is some kind of a miracle, you can forget about coming back to live with us again."

He was trapped. He was angry but unable to walk away. He snarled, "You know you should be a Billy Graham!" "No, I am who God wants me to be. And you have just heard what He wanted me to tell you." He was so glad when we got to my home. He left without another word.

At Christmas that year, Dr. Berman said to me, "We see the strain in your face. Why don't you take the children to visit with your family?" Then they loaned me airfare to take the children to Georgia for a visit with my parents! I thank God for giving me such good neighbors. My first prayer request to God after Randy left this time was "Lord, would You please be a father to my children? You know I can't be both a father and a mother; in fact, I can't even be a mother unless you teach me how. Please teach me how to be a mother, and would You be their father?" Gradually, I began to regain my sense of direction.

Chapter 29

1971: CALLED to be a TEACHER

There were approximately 26 children in my first grade class. It was a truly diverse mix, but predominately middle-class African Americans and Jews. Both groups of parents were aggressive and demanded to be involved in their children's education. Most of the time I welcomed their help; sometimes it was necessary to disagree with them. Once a Jewish parent quizzed me two or three times weekly about her son's progress. I had noticed nothing special about the little boy. He was quite playful; that was not unusual. However, this mother wanted conferences all the time. I showed her work samples and asked, "What are you looking for?" She replied, "I just want to know how he is doing in his science and social studies. I can see that he is doing well in reading and math." I obliged her, I thought.

Later that evening at dinner I told my children about this parent who was usurping almost as much of my time as her son was. Doug asked, "Mom, is that Mrs. Clard's son?" "I don't know, Doug. His name is Les Clard" "Mom, don't you remember that Mrs. Clard was my 7th grade English teacher?"

I really didn't remember, but Doug prompted me by recalling an incident that happened during his first year in high school. When Doug entered Walnut Hills High School, I attended the first Open House at the school. The format was to have the parents visit their child's classes as a way of showing what their child experienced that day. Doug's English class met at the seventh bell in an Army barracks. There was a social studies class next door; a curtain separated the two classes. The social studies teacher had a booming voice; Mrs. Clard had a soft voice. It was necessary to strain to hear her voice over his. At the end of the period, she invited parents to look at his/her child's class record. When I saw Doug's record, I asked her, "Why did you give Doug a C on his report card? All of the papers he brought home had grades of A or B." I could see that she was grasping for an answer. I guessed that in her prejudice she automatically believed that a black child could not do A and B work. Yet, in her grade book he had all A's and B's. She blushed and started talking fast.

"I prefer to grade up rather than down." "What does that mean?" "Well, if the child gets a better grade as the year progresses, I prefer to give a higher grade." "But what if he improves consistently? How do you justify giving him a C when all of his work thus far has been A's and B's?" She had no answer.

At the end of the evening, the principal stood near his door to accept compliments from parents about their child's progress. When I reached him, I asked, "Why is the 7th bell English class housed next to the social studies class in the barracks?"

He immediately asked me into his office. He closed the door and asked, "How may I help you?" I told him about my conversation with Mrs. Clard adding, "Why would a class that is as important as English be placed in a hot barracks at the seventh bell? And the English teacher's voice is drowned out by the voice of the social studies teacher." He said, "Well, someone has to be scheduled at that time, so your son happens to be in that class."

However, at the next grading period, the teacher gave him a grade of A; in fact the remainder of his grades from her that year were all A's.

Now Doug said, "Perhaps Mrs. Clard thinks that you are going to treat Les the way she treated me." "God would not allow me to mistreat a child because of his or her ethnicity."

The remainder of the year went well. I never alluded to the fact that I remembered Mrs. Clard as Doug's English teacher. Her son did well. She was so pleased, she requested that her daughter also be assigned to me as her first grade teacher.

There were many children at the school who needed special help. One was a little boy who was assigned to me because he lacked self-control. The principal at another school asked Mrs. Whittaker to take this child because there was no teacher at her school who was capable of containing him. He was perhaps the brightest child I ever taught. At age six, he could ride all over the city alone on the bus. He was fearless, but vulnerable. At our first meeting Charlie announced, "All teachers are dumb; none of them can teach me anything."

I didn't exactly dismiss his comments but I didn't give them too much weight either. On his first day with the class, I was working with a small group when Charlie got up, and without a word to me, walked out of the room. My dilemma was: "Do I leave the whole class and go after Charlie, or ignore Charlie and remain with the class?"

The school was located at a dangerous intersection and there was no crossing guard on duty at this time of day. So I said to the class, "I need to go get Charlie. Please stay in your seats and continue your work."

I caught up with Charlie as he left the building. I took his hand and knelt down so my eyes were level with his. "Charlie, you may not walk out of the class without permission. I had to leave all your classmates to come after you. We will go back to class now, and you are to remain in the classroom until recess. At that time, all of us will go out to play." "But I already know all that stuff you are talking about. I can read anything. I don't need to go to school."

Holding his hand, we went back into the classroom. Charlie was now seated near me, in case he tried to leave the class again. On the playground, he refused to play with the other children. He preferred to be close to me. I urged him to go and play with the other children. "No, they don't like me; they won't play with me." He seemed fascinated by the girls jumping rope. I said to him, "Go and ask the girls to teach you how to jump rope." "Do you think they will let me?" "Go and ask them."

They welcomed him gladly, but teaching him how to jump was not easy. However, at this age, children aren't aware that there are things they can't do. The girls believed they could teach him. And the ice was broken. At subsequent recess periods, the girls would call to Charlie to come and jump rope with them. They were very patient with him.

Another day, following recess, we were doing directed handwriting. The letter we worked on that day was "C". Directed handwriting was a lesson I taught with the use of an overhead projector. My transparency duplicated the children's writing paper. As I explained how to write the capital C, Charlie exclaimed, "So that's how you write that letter!" "Yes, Charlie. That letter is called capital C. The lower case c is made the same way, but it is smaller, and starts at the red line and goes down to the bottom blue line."

Charlie was hooked. He came up to me and asked, "Will you teach me how to write my name?" "I certainly will, Charlie." I also taught him how to write his name in cursive. After this he was convinced that he knew everything, and therefore did not need to come to school.

Charlie was right about not needing to be taught how to read; his reading was far advanced to the other students; but he had other needs. He didn't know how to tie his shoelaces and he needed lots of help with social skills. It was necessary for me to customize some of his instruction. He enjoyed classical music, and understood a lot about it. I converted the doll corner into a learning station for him. In the station, I placed a record player with records, earphones, and a tape recorder. Charlie could operate the record player and the tape recorder. Because he couldn't write his impressions of the music, he recorded his report to me. He told me who wrote the music and he gave his impression of how it sounded. At noon, while eating lunch, I would listen to his report and record comments to him.

I used this same method to accommodate a kindergartener who could read but could not complete follow-up writing assignments. Bridgette was sent to my room for reading only because the kindergarten teacher did not have enough children to form a reading group. Bridgette would meet with the reading group for instruction, but when I gave follow-up assignments to the other group members, she was sent to the recording corner to continue reading and to record her comprehension of the story. I listened to her report and made comments to her as well. At one time during the year, I was actually preparing for seven different reading levels. What a challenge! Thank God it only lasted one year.

In both cases I had satisfactory results. On the playground one day, Charlie exclaimed to another teacher, "Mrs. Hooker is the best teacher in the world!" "Charlie, how many teachers have you had?" I asked. "Two. But you are the best teacher in the world."

Charlie became involved in drama and theater. In 1993, when I was named an Enquirer Newspaper Woman of the Year, his mother called to thank me again for the way I had helped him. In response to my question about Charlie, she told me he was working for television in Cleveland.

No one knew how Bridgette had learned to read. She came from a single family home, and had a little brother. Her mother could not answer my question, so I decided to ask Bridgette. She said that she learned to read by watching Sesame Street on television. With further questioning she explained that she learned the sounds of the letters and remembered what she learned each day. That was remarkable! I requested that she be tested for a gifted class. She truly was gifted, and went on to make great strides in school. Her little brother, Jason, on the other hand, was a normal little boy. He had not taught himself to read; neither had his sister helped him learn to read.

I have many satisfying stories like this. Nothing gives me more pleasure than to help a child discover his/her innate abilities. Although I retired 12 years ago in 1990, I continue to tutor reading in a local public school.

Chapter 30

1972: LAUNCHING the HOOKER Children: First, Doug

My satisfaction extended to helping my own children achieve success in their lives. In 1972, Doug graduated from high school. I had been praying about how to pay for his college expenses. He had been accepted to Georgia Tech, and I had no money to send him there. At the kitchen sink one day – I talked with God a lot at the kitchen sink – I prayed, "Lord, how am I going to pay Doug's college expenses? He is a good student and he deserves a chance to go to college. But how will I pay for it? Should I take a second mortgage on the house? I don't know what to do. Please help me."

The telephone rang. "Mrs. Hooker, this is the Internal Revenue. Your income tax has come up for audit." The caller continued telling me what to bring with me when I came for the hearing. I collected all the information and went to be audited.

The woman interviewing me could tell that I was tense. She began by trying to help me relax. As she examined the papers I handed her, she asked, "Do you get alimony?" "No." "Not even one dollar?" "No." "Why? Usually, the wife is granted at least one dollar." "I didn't want it." "Do all the children live with you? And are you the sole support for their care?" "Yes." "Does Mr. Hooker claim any of them?" "No, he shouldn't." "Has he asked you to allow him to claim at least two of them?" "Yes. I refused." "Do you get child support?" "Yes." "Who prepared your taxes?" "I did." "Well, Mrs. Hooker, you included the child support in your earnings. Child support is not taxable. The IRS owes you $2000.00 plus interest." Thank You, Heavenly Father! I came home and called my mother to tell her what had happened. Her response was "God even makes us save money for ourselves."

I called Randy and asked him to take Doug shopping for a suit; this was to be his first dress suit. Randy and Doug picked out a dark blue suit with pinstripes. My, he looked handsome and grownup, too. After Doug outgrew the suit, David wore it for a while.

Randy helped me drive Doug to Atlanta to enroll at Georgia Tech. I gave Doug a money order for $1,000. It would have to last him until we could get some more. I was happy that Doug was able to go to college, but I experienced depression for nearly a year after he left the house. He had been such a strong support for me. However, I realized I still had four more children to help get into and through college. One reason Doug and I wanted him to go to Georgia Tech was that he could begin his co-op assignment in the second semester of his freshman year, and get paid for working outside the university. The Marta Transit System hired him for three years. He worked hard, and paid his own expenses until his fourth year. During the summer break after his junior year he came home and said, "Mom, may I talk with you?" He came into my bedroom and he was crying. "Mom, I'm going to have to drop out of school." "Why, Son?" "Mom, do you realize I have been wearing the same underwear for four years?" "Wear them for one more year, Doug. Then you will be able to buy us all underwear."

David had four hundred dollars in his college savings account. I gave that to Doug and sent him back to Atlanta. It lifted his spirits so! His only outerwear was a plaid shirt with a flannel lining. I had been unable to buy him a calculator. "Doug, you will have to compute your problems in your head. In the long run, you will be better off for it." We were struggling, but I tried to keep priorities in perspective.

From his experiences, I decided to do the same thing for the others. Each was given help to start school; then, as they were struggling in the final year, I gave them a big bonus. Each of them worked and helped pay his/her own expenses for college. Doug received his Mechanical Engineering degree from Georgia Tech in 1978, and a master's in Technology and Science Policy in 1985. He is married to Patrise Perkins Hooker, a lawyer who has her own law firm. He also earned a master's degree in Business Administration from Emory University. He has had some impressive jobs, among them serving as Commissioner of Public Works of Atlanta for six years. He is now a vice president of a national engineering consulting firm. He and Patrise have served on the Georgia Tech Alumni Association Board of Trustees. Patrise also earned two master's degrees from Emory after earning an engineering degree from Georgia Tech: (an MBA and Juris Doctor). They are the parents of two of my three grandchildren. Doug practiced the lesson Granddaddy Anderson taught by example; he has always owned his own home.

Chapter 31

1975: MY TIME to RETURN to SCHOOL

After Doug departed into college, my career began to take off. In 1974 while working at North Avondale Elementary School, I met a professor from the University of Wisconsin – Eau Claire. We met at the University of Cincinnati. Dr. Joyal had been a presenter at a workshop at UC, which I was attending. We sat at the same table for lunch. During the conversation, he commented that he had gone all the way through school – even to earning a Ph.D. – and had never met one African American.

"Where did you go to school?" I asked. "In Eau Claire, Wisconsin." "And you never met any African Americans?" "No, except on television. We have none on our campus now."

This was almost unbelievable to me. So I said, "I'm coming up there to integrate that place for you!" He picked up on the offer immediately, and asked, "Would you?' "Well you need someone to do it. Imagine, in 1974 a college campus in the United States with no African Americans."

I thought no more of the conversation, but the next week I was called out of class to answer the telephone. My first thought was of my children. I began praying that they were all right. It was Dr. Joyal: "Odessa, everything is all set. Can you come in two weeks?" I was surprised. "No, Dr. Joyal. I signed a contract to work this year." "Can you come next semester?" "I don't know. I'll let you know." My big mouth and me! What had I gotten myself into now?

The 1974-75 school year began well. I was asked to be a learning community leader. Our community was comprised of 150 – 175 children, grades kindergarten – second grade; 5 teachers; an instructional assistant; one student teacher, and a secretary. The building where we were housed was a satellite campus of North Avondale Elementary. It was located approximately one mile from the main school building. The Board of Education had rented classrooms in a church. There was no administrator, so I unofficially served as principal. The student teacher was also assigned to me. My duties included teaching in a multi aged classroom, doing demonstration teaching, supervising the personnel assigned to the community, coordinating contributions of extra school personnel, and serving as liaison for intra/inter-unit communication. This extra work carried no additional pay or title.

Because I still needed to spend time with my biological children, I prioritized my responsibilities and divided my day accordingly. The workday was 7:30 – 5:00 Monday through Friday. I vowed to take no schoolwork home. Everything that could not be completed at work in one day could wait until the next day. I was unable to participate in any extra curricula activities.

Dr. Joyal was still interested in my visit to the University of Wisconsin – Eau Claire for the second semester, so I began making arrangements. The first priority in my planning involved the children in my class; I could not leave them in the middle of the school year unless my replacement was a competent person with whom they were familiar. My student teacher that year was a natural teacher. In my whole career, I have only known one other young teacher who was as competent. Denise Hewitt was due to graduate in January 1975; I had to leave January 1975. My principal arranged for her to replace me; the children knew her well and she knew them. So, I traveled to Eau-Claire Wisconsin in January to attend the University of Wisconsin- Eau Claire, full scholarship, and stipend provided.

Mrs. Smith moved in with my children. This assured me that they would receive proper care. I also asked Randy to move in with them. I rationalized this would give him an opportunity to really get to know them – and they him. And, it would assure that they had at least one parent at home. In return, he was to pay the utilities and buy groceries.

Darrell was in kindergarten. He was accustomed to having me read to him each night. At this time, his favorite story was *Little House in the Big Woods*, by Laura Ingalls Wilder. Before I left for Eau Clare, I taped the story, chapter by chapter. I also taped a few more stories. Each night while I was away, Margaret played a story or a chapter for him.

I had budgeted my income to be able to pay the mortgage every month, the other bills, and Mrs. Smith. I gave up my leased car. I made detailed arrangements for the children's care, but I wasn't prepared for how the separation would affect me. I missed them so much! It was necessary to will myself to remain in Wisconsin through the second week. During the day I would concentrate on studying, but I missed them so much at night. Every night, tears came to my ears.

And the children missed me. Using my stipend, I sent them gifts. I wrote to them every week. Melanie took the responsibility of forwarding their mail to me. I didn't have money to call them long distance.

For spring break, I had two weeks off. Immediately, I went home. Randy met me at the bus station, but he hardly spoke. My first concern were the children. "How are they doing?" "You'll soon be home and you can see for yourself." He refused to come into the house. Indeed, I did see for myself! Mrs. Smith and Darrell met me before I could reach the house. Darrell was so weak he could hardly stand. The other children came to hug and kiss me, too. They were so happy to have me home. "Mrs. Smith, what is wrong with Darrell?" I asked as I took him into my arms. "Mrs. Hooker, I told Mr. Hooker he was sick, but he didn't do anything about it." As we came into the house, they all started talking at once. They had so much to tell me.

A visit to the doctor revealed that Darrel was suffering from a number of allergies. He was prescribed an antihistamine, and his symptoms subsided.

When I examined the mail, I discovered that Randy had not paid the utilities; I was being threatened for cut-off. There was very little food in the house. I also learned that Randy had taken a job cleaning professional buildings at night. He was never at home when the children were awake. They would leave notes for him, but he did not respond. They were so frustrated. Mrs. Smith had not called or written to tell me because she didn't want to worry me.

Melanie said, "Mom, how did you put up with Dad as long as you did? He didn't help us at all!" I prayed, "Help me, Heavenly Father!"

As soon as my break ended, I returned to Appleton and Fond du Lac Wisconsin to complete my two week assignments there. Then I went on to Eau Claire. My first question to my professors was this: "You say that this program, IGE (Individually Guided Education) allows a person to work at his or her own pace, so if I finish the program requirements I may leave?" "That's correct, Odessa." "O. K. I need to get home to see about my children, so I want permission to leave before the semester is officially ended, if I can finish." "That's fine with us."

I worked day and night, and within two weeks I submitted all my assignments and was granted permission to leave. I earned five A's, and received all my credits. I returned home the first week in May 1975. I had no money, so I called my principal and asked her to call me for any substitute assignments that might be needed. Her response pleased me. "Dessa, your call is just in time. Rosa will have to begin her maternity leave early; I need someone to take her class for the rest of the year."

Now I had at least one month of income. Meanwhile, two professors from Miami University were trying to market a new math program in the Cincinnati Public Schools. They were offering stipends to any teacher who would take the four weeks in-service to learn a program titled DMP, Developmental Mathematical Processes. I signed up. That was one more month of income.

Fortunately, both options took place at North Avondale Elementary School. I walked the five blocks to work each day. Some of the school supervisors learned of my IGE training and asked me to make presentations for some of the local schools. I was paid for these services throughout the month of July.

In August, I received a call from my principal. "Dessa, I have been asked by some Wright State Professors to do a workshop about IGE. I can't go. Can you go in my place?" "Nikki, I think they want a principal; that's why they asked you." "But you know more about IGE than I do." "How much does it pay, Nikki?" "$300.00 per hour." "I can do that."

The school was in Cleveland, Ohio. I knew that the woman who was my matron of honor for my wedding worked in the Cleveland Public Schools. I called her, told her about the assignment, and asked if she could meet me at the bus station and let me lodge with her for a few days. She was delighted to help. Mrs. Smith was off for the summer,

120

but she came and stayed with the children. I took a bus to Cleveland; Sally Clare met me and took me to the school the next day. I greatly enjoyed the visit with her. We talked late into the night about people and conditions in Barnesville; she was a gracious hostess. She also took me back to the bus station. And I had enough money to get us through August and even buy a few new school clothes for the children. I also did a few more workshops in IGE and DMP. In September, I leased a car as the new school year began.

I was assigned again to North Avondale. There was one unfinished item: the children needed some counseling to overcome the damage experienced by my absence and the effects of their dad's lack of attention to them. My insurance helped cover the cost of the counseling. At one point, the counselor wanted Randy to come with the family. I invited him. The session was revealing. I was already accustomed to Randy always painting me in a bad light. He seemed to think that was his role. But now, Melanie and David felt free to express their opposition to my parenting techniques because their dad was there to support them. Somehow everything negative that the children had experienced was my fault. Margaret was the youngest, but she completely disagreed with them. She thought mommy was doing a good job. I did not try to defend myself; instead I accepted their criticism; but I knew that I was doing the best I could. As we were leaving the session, Melanie said, "We were pretty hard on you in there, weren't we Mom?"

"No, I think you gave your honest opinion; I accept your critique. However, I shall continue to make the best decisions I can as your only parent, and pray that you are not permanently damaged by my parenting."

The next challenge was a financial one. The roof sprang a leak. Where would I get money to pay for a new roof? As usual, I consulted with God. I should call and get three estimates and go from there. This was something new for me; I needed guidance. But I called, and I got three estimates. I chose the company that was located near our home. They were reputable, but they were also accessible; if the work was less than satisfactory, I could reach them readily.

One day the school secretary came to the door and said I had a telephone call. "Please take a message, Jan. I will return the call at a more convenient time." She insisted, "I'll watch the class." The caller was Professor Jim LaPlant whom I had met earlier at the University of Cincinnati. He wanted to know if I would teach a course that summer at the university. The title was "Individualizing Mathematics in the Elementary School." My standard question at this time was "How much does it pay?" "Two thousand, five hundred dollars for the two weeks. You may have an assistant who will be paid one thousand dollars. All materials and supplies will be furnished," he said. Again God surprised me. The cost to replace my roof was two thousand, five hundred dollars!

My math strength was at the primary level, so I asked a strong middle grade math teacher, Naomi Clark to be my assistant. She had lots of materials, and a lot of expertise. She was a great help. I taught the class, collected my pay, and gave it to the roofers.

Chapter 32

1975: LAUNCHING the HOOKER Children: Second, Melanie

Melanie's teen years were turbulent. She often disagreed with my decisions; we were often at odds. She didn't like my choices of clothing for her. There was little money to spend on clothes, but she always had enough clothes to look well, I thought. We also disagreed on her social life. She wanted to date early. I said no. She persisted, "Mom, how old were you when you and daddy began to date?" "We didn't date alone until we were seniors in high school," was my reply. " It seems to me your Auntie Pearl was with us then."

At age 13 she had been selected to be in a Daisy Chain, something like a pre-debutante. We argued about her dress. I made her a simple white sheath dress, the requirement stipulated by the planners. I thought she looked so pretty, but she refused to wear the dress after the ceremony. I took it back and wore it myself. Even when she was a baby, I made most of her clothes- Margaret's, too. It was quite a saving, and it meant they could have a few more clothes than they could have had otherwise. Melanie always complained. However, when I made a jumpsuit for myself, she was eager to wear it. I realized she was unsure of herself, but she trusted my judgment about my clothes.

Melanie was thirteen years old when Darrell was born. Following his birth, she showed signs of depression. I thought it might help her to get away from the family, so I scraped enough money to send her for a visit with my sister in California. Oreatha was much younger than I was; perhaps she could identify with Melanie's problems. The other children were not envious of the special treat for Melanie; instead, they were happy for her.

Upon return, she brought a gift to me: a blue glass bell. I still cherish it. It signified to me that she loved me and thought about me when she was away from home.

Her depression continued however. I admit I wasn't smart enough to arrange counseling for her. I really believed that she was surly because she couldn't get her way. When her complaints spilled over into the physical realm, my obstetrician prescribed pain medicine for her monthly cycle. I realized that she was quite sedentary, and slightly overweight. I encouraged her to be more active physically. One day while at work I received a call from her school. Melanie was ill and I needed to come and get her. When I arrived, she looked so surly! I said to her, "Come on Mel. Let's go home."

I didn't realize what was happening to her. A visit to the doctor revealed that she had taken too much of her pain medication. She was hospitalized at Children's Hospital. She requested that her daddy visit her. My presence was not requested. Randy conveyed to me that she was going to be kept at the hospital for a time until the doctors could evaluate her. When she was released after two weeks she refused to live with us. She chose to live with her best friend's family. I had no problem with that until the mother of the family called me a month later to say she needed money to keep Melanie. I explained that I was financially unable to pay for separate upkeep for Melanie. So, she had to return home.

She was welcomed with open arms by her siblings and me. So after a while things were back to where they were before she left. I was surprised that she actually began to exercise and work at trying to lose weight. She jogged every day. I could see her slim down before my very eyes. Melanie was in her senior year while I was away at the University of Wisconsin-Eau Care. She had struggled to make arrangements to apply to college, and she needed one of her parents to help her. She was angry that neither of us was available when she needed help. I was proud of her though; she had been quite mature in the matter. With the help of her counselor, she had received a scholarship to Chatham College in Pittsburgh. She left for college the following September. After her second year at Chatham, It was necessary for her to return home and finish her degree at the University of Cincinnati.

At age 19, she requested – and was granted – permission to move into her own apartment. She struggled but managed to remain independent after leaving home. She eventually earned a bachelor's and a master's degree in Communications. In 1987, Melanie married. We were all thrilled with the beautiful wedding. After a nine-year marriage, she and her husband separated. He died a few years later.

124

Chapter 33

1976: LAUNCHING the HOOKER Children: Third, David

David too began exhibiting some teenage problems. A friend of mine gave him an after school job. That helped a little. When he was younger, he had been assigned Scripture verses to memorize and every morning before he left for school we would pray together and ask God to help him get through the day. We discussed what part of the day was the roughest. I promised to pray for him at that time. Then, one day he came home with a note stating that he had been suspended from school. I went to meet with the assistant principal and one of his teachers. I was surprised at how young the teacher appeared. He told me that David was disrespectful in his class. Specifically, David would study Spanish instead of pay attention to the physical education teacher. Then he added, "I know David's daddy is not in the home, so I was trying to be a father figure for him." He continued, "David has rebuffed all my efforts to try to help him. Now, I hope I never have to see his face again!"

I snapped back "David doesn't need you to be his father. I'm sure if he had a choice he would not want to see your face again either. But you are supposed to be the adult. David is still a student. However, because he has no choice but to return to your class, I expect you to act like an adult. I promise you David will be respectful in your class."

To David I said, "You are expected to act as you have been taught to act. God expects you to act like His child, and I do, too. Remember Proverbs 10:1 "A wise son maketh a glad father; but a foolish son is the heaviness of his mother." A few weeks later, the teacher called me to report that David had been a perfect gentleman in his class. I thanked him, and complimented David on being the son I knew he could be.

When David was about fourteen be exhibited a concern for the less fortunate and physically challenged. His summer volunteer work was with a camp for the mentally challenged. Without being awakened on Saturday mornings, he would get up and walk more than a mile to get a bus to work at Camp Stepping Stone. The summer following high school graduation, he was paid to take four men to summer camp for

125

a week. He described the experience when he returned. "Mom, I was assigned these guys who were physically adult but their mental age was that of a child. I lived with them in a cabin. Each night it was impossible to get them to go to sleep at the same time. Whenever I would get one of them into bed, another one would walk away from the cabin. Then I had to get him back. This went on all night. I haven't had an hour of sleep for a whole week. I'm glad I had my Bible. I never needed it more than I did at that camp."

David was Darrell's hero; Darrell looked up to his older brother. Once I was summoned to court with David. The judge read the charges. "David, the officer reports that you were driving 72 miles per hour coming down Winton Road Hill. Is this true?" "Yes sir." The judge had been watching my face while he talked to David. I was very surprised to hear this. David had been allowed to drive the car on weekend nights because he had to close up at Ponderosa where he worked. I didn't want him to ride the bus after 2:00 am. The judge continued, "I believe your mother can handle this matter. You have no prior record, so I don't want to make it a hardship for you to work." Then the judge said to me, " Mrs. Hooker, I'm going to release David to you." "Thank you, Your Honor. I'm disappointed that David has shown this immaturity. His young brother idolizes him; this action is not what I want Darrell to mimic. I will handle the matter."

David had to give up the car keys and his privilege to drive for at least 4 weeks. I still didn't want him to ride the bus that late. Therefore, this was hard on me, too. I had to stay up Friday and Saturday nights to pick him up from work. David went on to graduate from high school. He earned a partial scholarship to Morehouse College. The year he graduated from Morehouse, he received a scholarship to study in the Dominican Republic and at Princeton. He was nominated to the college Who's Who In American Colleges and Universities. For one year after leaving Morehouse, he researched scholarships and grants, and has since gone on to earn four more degrees. He is a lawyer. After he graduated from U-Mass, Amherst, I was able to give him $2,000 for a gift. He bought a used Volvo, packed his belongings, and went directly to Washington, DC. That was where he always wanted to be. He had no job or job prospect, no money, and no housing. Whenever he called during the first two weeks, he had no telephone number or address at which he could be located. The third week he reported that he had run into a college classmate who lived there; Brian invited David to share his apartment until David could find a job

126

and his own living quarters. Living in DC was challenging. He had his car wheels locked by the police because he was parked in a neighborhood in which he was not a resident. His car proved to be a liability instead of an asset. He finally parked it in Virginia where he found work. He lived in DC for five years. While employed with the National Institute of Dispute Resolutions, he decided he wanted to go back to school to study law.

Again he researched scholarships and grants and won enough in grants to study law at Emory University. As before at the other schools he attended, he was very involved in student government. There are two plaques on my wall which he earned while at Emory. One reads: Who's Who Among Students in American Universities & Colleges- This is to certify that David Anderson Hooker has been elected to Who's Who Among Students in American Universities & Colleges in recognition of outstanding merit and accomplishment as a student at Emory University, 1993-1994. The other plaque reads: Emory University School of Law DISTINGUISHED SERVICE AWARD, 1994. David A. Hooker for his outstanding participation in the Law School's program of activities and in recognition of his many volunteer services in support of the student affairs of the law school.

David had served as president of his school's student body, just as his brother before him. He has gone on to serve five years with the Attorney General's Office in Atlanta, and with a prominent law firm. He was married briefly. Now he has his own practice; his business card reads: DAVID ANDERSON HOOKER, Mediator and Attorney-at-Law.

In recent years he has been sent to third world countries to conduct workshops in grass roots organizing, conflict resolution training, and mediation. In 2001, he returned to school at Emory to study for a theology degree. Following Granddaddy Anderson's advice, David too owns his home.

Chapter 34

1978: LAUNCHING the HOOKER Children: Fourth, Margaret

Our next child, Margaret had her share of challenges as she grew up. She always wanted to please others, especially her family, so she specialized in being conciliatory. Margaret was nine years old when Darrel was born. She seemed to welcome him, and she was his most sensitive baby sitter. But something else in her behavior expressed what she could not. Although very intelligent, her grades began to suffer with the disruptions in the family. When Margaret reached high school, she brought home her first report card. After that, she never allowed me to see another one. In her tenth grade year, she took herself out of Walnut Hills and registered at the City Wide Academy. This school was designed to allow students to complete coursework that was not necessarily confined to the classroom; the requirements were not tightly structured. Enrollees met for classes at different places in the city. Margaret studied science at the zoo, art at an art studio, and government downtown at city hall. But, she realized that there would not be a yearbook or formal graduation at this school, so she returned to Walnut Hills for her senior year. Because she had missed her junior year at Walnut Hills, she had to take a full load of classes to graduate. But she did. Then she decided she would not attend college.

All my children knew that they were allowed to stay home with mom until they finished college, but if they chose not to go to college, and wanted to live at home, they had to pay rent. Margaret is the only one who chose not to go to college immediately. She took a job at Shillito's, a downtown department store. She did not complain about paying rent either. When she was nineteen, she enrolled in school at the University of Cincinnati. After two years, she graduated with an associate liberal arts degree. I never pressured her to go on and earn a bachelor's degree, but I did say to her that I didn't think she would be happy for a lifetime by working as a retail store clerk.

I knew that even without a four-year college degree, she would be successful. She had always been a self-starter and an industrious person. When she was 14 years old, she initiated the move to acquire a work permit from the Board of Education. She seemed very happy working at Ponderosa as a waitress. Her work record is excellent. She is conscientious, hard working, and very pleasant. When she worked at Shillito's, she attracted customers who asked for her services. She was happy, but I knew she could do more.

One day, my sister said to me, "Dess, I think Margaret is going to college this year." "I don't think so. She hasn't mentioned it to me."

When I asked Margaret about her intentions, she said yes, she planned to enter Ohio University in the fall. "Margaret, you should at least let me know; I have to pay the bill." She went off to Ohio University, but came home after the first quarter. When she came home, she brought all her belongings. "Margaret, didn't they have some place you could store your things?" "I brought them because I don't plan to go back."

This time I did intervene. "Margaret, you will lose all the money you have paid and receive no credit. You should try for at least one year." She was a sensitive and obedient daughter. She just did not feel successful at studying. A few days before time to return to school she came into my room to talk with me. She sat on my lap, and blurted out, "Mom, do I have to go back to school?" She was crying. "Margaret, you owe it to yourself to try at least one year. Then, if you don't want to, you may come home. But give yourself a chance."

She went back, and resolved to complete the degree requirements. For a while, I wrote to her every day, encouraging her to give it her best shot. The following spring, she invited me to attend a parent day. I went and took my two young nieces and Darrell. She was so happy to see us.

Visiting at the school helped me understand why she might not want to stay. The girls in the dormitory were young and undisciplined. She took me into a room to meet a girlfriend. The girl's roommate and her boyfriend were actually having sex right in the room - oblivious of our presence. When I went to the restroom, some of the toilets were not flushed. I asked her if this was the norm. She said it was, and she felt like the dorm mother – cleaning up behind some of the younger girls and counseling some of them. I understood that Margaret was more mature than a number of the girls in the dormitory. She was serious about her studies; some of them were not. But God had blessed her with a wonderful roommate. They got along well together. Their friendship continues even now. She also became a friend with two young women. These friendships helped her complete her degree program. We were so proud of her when she graduated. I ordered a metal plate with her graduation information inscribed on it:

"The President of the Board of Trustees of the Ohio University announces the conferring of degrees Saturday morning June fifteenth nineteen hundred and eighty-five at ten o'clock, Convention Center, Athens, Ohio – Margaret Pauline Hooker, BS"

Several members of the family attended the graduation. Margaret was so pleased that she persevered. She came home and started looking for work. The jobs she found in her field, Health Education, were unsatisfactory, so she went back to work at the department store. But she was contented and so was I. She was so helpful and dependable. I tried hard not to expect that she would always be satisfied with staying home. She and Darrell got along so well together. Like her Grandmama Pauline, she showed selfless concern for him. He became dependent on her to be there for him.

Then, at age 27 Margaret met Jim at work. They became serious about each other. In December of that year, Jim asked my permission to marry Margaret. I was glad that they wanted to get married, but I asked Margaret to give me a year to recover from Melanie's wedding expenses. I'm sure they first meant to do so, but they announced their wedding soon thereafter. They were married in July 1988. Theirs was a beautiful wedding, too. The following December they moved to Chicago. Two years later their relationship was on the rocks. They separated and divorced, and Margaret returned home. She stayed home for one year while she studied at a local Culinary School. Then she went to work for Closson's Furniture and Design Store; she rose to become the chairman of the Design Studio. On weekends she worked as an independent caterer. That was also the year Darrell graduated from high school: Four down, one returned, and one to go.

Chapter 35

1988: LAUNCHING the HOOKER Children: Fifth, Darrell

While I was studying at the University of Wisconsin-Eau Claire, Darrell began experiencing challenges that required attention. He exhibited some anxiety problems. He wanted to know if I was going away again. I assured him that I was not. I tried to have him verbalize how he felt about my absence. "Did Margaret play the stories for you at night?" "Yes, Mommy, but that was not you! Where were you? I missed you." "Well, I am at home now to stay with you and David and Margaret."

However, his kindergarten experience had been disappointing. He had eagerly looked forward to going to school because he had witnessed his older siblings studying every night, and he wanted the experience, too. He had insisted that I teach him how to read so he would be ready for school. I had tried by recording chart stories that he dictated as he described pictures from magazines. We would hang the chart behind the closet door in his room. He enjoyed 'reading' the stories at bedtime. The transition to reading a book was not as successful. I didn't bother too much about it. He had had preschool experiences since age two. He was enrolled in the program at the university where he went two half days when he was two years old, three half days at age three, and four half days at age four. He could tie his shoes, button his shirt, and dress himself. He recognized his colors and letters of the alphabet. As well as I could discern he was much better prepared for kindergarten than the kindergartners I had taught. Yet, he told me when I returned, "Mommy, I don't think I want to go back to school next year." I became alarmed. "Oh my goodness, a kindergarten dropout!"

So, for the summer, I enrolled him in an enrichment program at the University of Cincinnati. And I said to his teacher, "I am not interested in having Darrell learn new skills; I want him to learn to like school."

He seemed to like it. We returned the next year – together. I was the learning community leader of the IGE community to which he was assigned. His teacher was one of the new teachers in my community. At one of our team meetings near the end of the year, she said, "I have three little boys who just can't catch on to reading. Could you take them for the last 10 weeks?"

I agreed. To my surprise, Darrell was one of the boys. They were all well behaved. They were attentive in the reading groups and they did their seatwork. However, each day was like starting all over again; they couldn't retain what had been previously taught. On the playground they were very coordinated; in fact, they were perhaps the best-coordinated boys in their age group. They could catch and throw balls and, they played well together. I consoled myself that he was just not ready to read.

There were two nuns in the class I taught that summer at the University of Cincinnati. They talked about their school. It sounded ideal. The largest class had 12 pupils. So I invited them to a cookout and asked if they thought I could get Darrell enrolled at Bethany for the next school year. It was arranged. There was just one catch: he would have to ride a school bus. I thought that if other children could ride to school, then he could, too. So, in grade two, Darrell rode the bus to school. The year went well. He began to learn to read. When he returned to the community school the next year, a series of unfortunate incidents challenged us again. He was bullied and named "Hooker Head."

I asked him to report this to his teacher. He did, but the bullying continued. I called the principal and the parents of the boys who had been identified as the perpetrators. The complaints subsided, so I assumed that things were going well.

One day, I received a letter stating that my presence was requested for a meeting with Darrell's teachers. I took a day off, and Darrell and I went to his school together. I was unprepared for the reports I got. I met with three teachers. They told me, "Darrell is a bully. He fights frequently, on the bus and on the playground. When it is time to line up to come in from recess, Darrell stands at the back of the line voluntarily and at a distance from the person in front of him. We think that Darrell has a chip on his shoulder, and will fight at the slightest provocation."

How shocking! I wondered, "Why haven't I been told of this before it reached this point? I have seen no evidence of the behavior you are describing to me." They said, " As a teacher we know that you have heard of parents who said they were unaware of their child's poor behavior."

"Yes, I have experienced that, but I am completely unaware of the behavior that you describe to me." The next question to me was, "What are you going to do about it?" "If you will get his things together, I'll take him home right now. I am angry that you have allowed this to go to an extreme without any prior notice to me." "But you can't take him out of school." "I disagree. Please get his things together and we will leave." "Where are you going to take him?" "I don't know, but we are leaving - now!"

When we got home, Darrell and I had a talk. I wasn't angry with him, but I needed his help to understand these accusations. "Darrell, tell me about school. You told me earlier in the year about the boys who were hitting you on the head. I thought that had stopped. " "It did for a while Mom, but they started again, so I began to hit back." "Why didn't you tell me? And what is this about you fighting on the playground? You never mentioned that to me."

"Mom, when I played soccer or football, they hit me so hard! And, when I fell on the ground, it hurt so much." "Then you would fight the person you thought had pushed you down? Darrell, I think you just enjoy fighting." "No, Mom! I stopped playing with the guys because they were so rough, but they still bothered me." He was crying. "All right. We will talk about it some more later. For now, you will have to go to school at Woodford Primary with me until we can figure out what to do."

The next week I took him to be evaluated. He was diagnosed with a learning disability. He could learn as well as other children but he needed to be taught differently. He had to be taught how to focus on his study and not be distracted so easily. And, he was tactually defensive; if someone hit him lightly, to him it felt like a hard blow. That explained why he learned to fight so readily. I was given an instrument to massage his arms and legs frequently. I enrolled him in a special school for children with learning disabilities. He was placed in a classroom with a few other students. The room was void of bright decorations like most primary classrooms. After the children met with their instructor to receive their assignments, each of them went to a cubicle to work. Even the lower half of the windows was covered with translucent paper. The instructor circulated among them, offering encouragement and help when needed. At a set time, they would regroup for another activity.

Darrell made progress at Springer School; he remained there for nearly two years. Then a specialist helped me choose a regular school to transfer him to. We decided on a public school directly across the street from the special school. He would be entering the fourth grade where normally, the children transitioned from a self-contained classroom to the circuit. At the school that we chose, Roselawn Condon, he would remain with one teacher all morning for most of his academic subjects, then in the afternoon, he traveled with other students to fine arts, physical education, and maybe one other subject. These arrangements precluded having him thrown completely on the circuit where he would have had to relate to several teachers in one day. And, because the school was across the street from the special school he had attended, he could possibly visit his former teacher to whom he was very attached.

The transition went well. He exhibited very good study skills and was quite capable of doing the work. At the end of the year, his teacher called me and said she was recommending him to the college prep tract. I was pleased. Darrell was apprehensive. He felt he was not ready for such a move. I said, "Your teacher would not have recommended you if she didn't think you could do the work." Gradually, he gained confidence and moved ahead. He even played in the school band for a while. At the end of 6th grade, he passed the test for admission to the college prep high school, Walnut Hills; but he chose to attend Roger Bacon, a parochial school. The proximity of that school to our house would allow him to walk to and from school and participate in after school activities. He remained there through 11th grade. Then, quite suddenly, he decided he wanted to graduate from the same high school his siblings had graduated from. I was strongly opposed to the idea. At Walnut Hills, he would receive no prompting or support from the teachers; he would be on his own. When we went to enroll at Walnut Hills, the counselor also told him that no one would prompt him about his progress; he would be on his own. This did not deter Darrell.

The change however proved to be more than he could handle. He struggled to retain his self-confidence, and do the work. For the first time, he became more interested in his clothes than in his grades; he fell so far behind, he wanted to drop out of school. Because he had made the decision, I allowed him to handle the consequences.

One morning, he called me at work. "Mom, why didn't you wake me before you left for work?" "Darrell, you have an alarm clock. I haven't been waking you for school before, why should I start now?"

He was really struggling. Until he transferred to Walnut Hills, he never watched television at night. He blamed me for causing him to miss out on what other kids were doing. In order to graduate, he would have to go to summer school his last year. Unknown to me, he had taken an action that dictated that he graduate from high school; he volunteered for the Marines. I was only aware of this move when I received a letter from the recruitment officer congratulating me on a fine son who tested drug free and had no prior court record.

I was flattered but surprised. It never occurred to me that he might have a court record or take drugs. None of his siblings had done such things; I expected him to do his best at all times. Doug was calling every week. He wanted to know if he should arrange to come for Darrell's graduation. I referred him to Darrell. Doug, too, wanted to blame me. "Mom, are you going to allow Darrell to drop out of school?" "Doug, Darrell has to make his own decision. If he chooses to fail, he must live with the decision. "

Unknown to both of us, Darrell was attending recruitment classes every Saturday. He would ask me to drop him off at the mall, and I did. But I didn't know what he was doing at the mall. However, to be accepted into the Marines, he had to graduate from high school. At the last minute, Doug arranged to come overnight to be present at Darrell's graduation. He received a blank diploma; he would get the real thing upon successful completion of summer school. After graduation, Darrell was sent to Parris Island for Marine boot training.

The new recruits were not allowed to write home immediately. When they were given permission to write, it was a form postcard. They had to report that they were doing fine. Later, I got a letter in which Darrell explained that he had passed every test except swimming. He was kept in the pool six or seven hours per day; a Marine has to know how to swim! Darrell had taken swim lessons for several years but had been unable to learn. He didn't like the feel of water on his skin. I had finally hired a private swim tutor, who helped Darrell progress to the point of not being fearful in the water. Now, he had no choice. If he was going to successfully complete boot camp, he had to learn to swim. In his letter, he said, "Pray for me, Mom." I knew then that he was in trouble, but I also knew that God could deliver him.

At last the invitation came to witness graduation from boot camp.

David was living in DC at the time. He wanted to know if I planned to go to Darrell's graduation from boot camp. Of course I was going! When I told David I planned to drive to Parris Island, South Carolina, he flew down to the Cincinnati- Northern Kentucky Airport. I picked him up there and we drove together to South Carolina. We lodged with one of my brothers-in-law and his wife who lived only a few miles away from Parris Island.

David and I were told that we might find Darrell at the canteen. We were both surprised when we saw him. He stood at least a head above most of the recruits. David saw him first. "Mom, that looks like Darrell's head over there."

Immediately I noticed that he was sick with fever. After he greeted us, I said, "Darrell, why didn't you go to sick bay? " He responded, "Mom, if I go to sick bay, I'll have to stay here two more weeks. There's no way I'm going to do that if I can help it."

The camp was indeed situated on an island – surrounded by alligators! The only way out was through the gate, unless you chose to take a chance with the alligators. Darrell told some horror stories about men who had tried to escape. He was laughing when he told them, so I took them lightly.

After the ceremony, we packed the car to drive home. Darrell slept on the back seat on top of his gear. He snored so loudly, the car shook. David said, "Mom, you are listening to one tired Marine." Darrell slept for hours as we drove back to Cincinnati.

Boot training had prevented Darrell's enrollment to college. The next year, he enrolled at Tuskegee Institute in Alabama. As the first semester ended, he was called to duty. He was sent to Saudi Arabia for Desert Storm. Communication from him was sparse. Once he called me to say that each soldier had twenty minutes to talk. They had come in from the war field to bathe and get a break before returning. He sounded cheerful enough. Anyway, there was nothing I could do except pray and wait. And that's what I did. I knew that God is everywhere, and if God chose to bring him home safely, I would see him alive again; if not, wherever he was, God was. So I was not anxious about his stay there.

After his return, he told interesting stories, but he didn't linger on his wartime experiences. He was too glad to be home again safely.

He had received credit for one semester of college, but he chose not to return to Tuskegee University. Instead, he went to Atlanta, so he could be near his brothers. David, who had relocated to Atlanta to study law at Emory, took the lead at getting Darrell into school. One day he called me to tell what the other family members had committed to contribute to Darrell's schooling. "What will you pledge to commit, Mom?" "David, I'm going to pay his tuition." "Really, Mom? That's great. Now all the bases are covered."

My senior daughter-in-law led the team of lawyers who supervised the merger of Atlanta University and Clark College, so she helped Darrell get into Clark Atlanta University. He liked some of the courses, and some he didn't. He was most disgruntled about the long lines at registration time. He finally dropped out and went to work. In 1996, he married LaTonya Frazier whom he met in Atlanta. After 6 years, they have a daughter, Darrell McKenna, my third grandchild.

Thank You, Lord! My children are all liberated and self-sufficient. You answered my prayer to be a father to them. You did a good job. I have no memorable negative memories about their growing up.

Chapter 36

1983: DRAFTED into ADMINISTRATION

Following the completion of my studies at the University of Wisconsin – Eau Claire in1975, as I sought to launch my children, I returned to the classroom and taught six, seven, and eight year-olds in a multi grade classroom. I had the opportunity to put my specialized educational training into practice. Then, in 1983 I was drafted into administration. Pearline and I were returning from vacation with Mama and Daddy. We stopped in Atlanta to visit with our brother, Kenneth (K. O.) who asked me, "Do you know Joe Ireland?" "Yes, he is Director of Personnel of the Cincinnati Public Schools." "Well, he called here trying to reach you." K. O. teases a lot, so I didn't take his comment seriously. But I wondered how he knew Joe Ireland. "I'm serious, Odessa. He called here and asked me to have you call him as soon as you get here." "How did he know I was coming here?"

"He called Dad, and Dad told him you would be stopping here on your way back to Cincinnati." "Well, it's too late to call now. Anyway, I'm on my way back to Cincinnati. I'll call him when I get there." Pearline and I left Atlanta early the next morning; we arrived in Cincinnati about 5:00 p.m. Margaret ran out to the car to meet us, saying, "Mom, call Mrs. Whittaker immediately!" As I entered the house, I asked Margaret what was happening. She explained, "Mrs. Whittaker has been trying to reach you for two days. I gave her Granddaddy Anderson's number. She called him and he told her that you had just left, but you would be stopping in Atlanta overnight." I dialed Nikki. "Dessa, call Vella Ellis, the Area Director right away, We have been trying to reach you. It is very important. Call right now." I dialed the number she gave me. "Mrs. Ellis, this is Odessa Hooker. Mrs. Whittaker told me to call you right away."

"O thank you. Mrs. Hooker, we would like you to become assistant Principal at Rockdale Elementary. You will start immediately, so please give me your answer now." "Mrs. Ellis, Pearline and I just got home. We came back early to prepare our classrooms. Anyway, I can't work at Rockdale. The Board has a policy that doesn't allow members of the same family to work together." "You have a family member who works at Rockdale?" "Yes. Pearline is my sister." "Pearline Riggins is your sister? I didn't know that. But I have a good

138

position for Pearline. Will you accept the position at Rockdale if Pearline agrees to move?" "Call her first, please. I can not answer until she accepts your proposed move."

Mrs. Ellis called me back almost immediately. "Mrs. Hooker, your sister says she will accept the new school. Will you accept Rockdale?" "Yes, I suppose so. But I need time to take care of my classroom." "Please report to Mr. Perry tomorrow. I'll call him tonight to let him know to expect you."

And that is how I was drafted into administration. Initially, I was assigned the position part-time. After a brief interview, the principal handed me a ring of several keys. There was no time to orient me to my duties; they sort of emerged as the principal saw fit. Our styles of work conflicted. I like orderly planning; he seemed overwhelmed by his responsibilities.

Nevertheless, I set goals for myself. He assigned me to oversee the primary grades; he would take the intermediate ones. I met with the primary teachers, grade by grade. At the first meeting, I discussed with them the previous year's standardized test scores the children had received. The people who had scored the tests also made comments about the condition of the test booklets. Unfortunately, Pearline's class results were included with the first grade teachers. I shared with each teacher the comments made by the scorers. Pearline had been complimented for the attention paid to details before submitting booklets for her class. There were critical comments about the other teachers.

Then I told the teachers that I had been assigned to work with them as a group. Using the test results as a starting point, I wanted to observe in each classroom and share with them my observations. "Do you want to give me an observation date and time or should I come to your rooms without an appointment?"

I was received with mixed attitudes: some of the teachers were happy to have my expertise; others were not. There was a perception that I had replaced Pearline, a peer whom they depended on. She had served unofficially as a lead teacher. Now, I was coming in as an administrator.

The children were out of control - partially because of inconsistent application of rules. Sometimes their inappropriate behavior was winked at; other times it met with harsh disapproval. I wanted to bring consistency and reality to the discipline the children received.

In a staff meeting one day, the principal stated, "Mrs. Hooker, you have been accused of emptying classrooms." "Let me see if I understand what you mean. Have I been accused of taking children out of their classrooms?" "No," one teacher responded. "But when we send children to you to be disciplined, you send them home." "I will respond to that accusation. When you send children to me to be disciplined, you are saying to the children, 'I can't control you; I will let someone else do it.' Then you send them to me. There are no baby sitting services in the office. When a child is in school, he should be with a teacher or a chaperone. If you can't control them in the classroom, the place for them is at home. If you don't send them to me, I won't send them home."

They got the message. My record keeping revealed that the same children were being sent to the office by the same teachers at the same time of day. When I shared my findings with the principal, he decided to see for himself if that was true. At a subsequent staff meeting, he read his findings to the teachers. Surely enough, my findings were validated. But the teachers felt they were unfairly singled out. I offered to work with them to help improve classroom discipline. Gradually, fewer children were sent to the office to be disciplined.

I preferred working directly with the children. One winter day I was granted that opportunity. The weather was severely cold. Many of our teachers needed substitutes. One of these substitutes called to say that she was unable to get to the school because of bad road conditions. I was asked to take a physical education class until another substitute teacher could be found. It was a fifth grade class. When I entered the room, all of the children recognized me. I said to them "I will work with you until a substitute teacher can get here. Because I can't teach gym, we will remain in the classroom and do another lesson instead. Please get prepared to write a letter." "A letter!" "Yes. I want you to describe to a student in another school what it is like to spend a day at Rockdale Elementary. Let's begin with the parts of a letter. How should it begin?" Someone reluctantly volunteered, "A return address."

"Good. What is the address of Rockdale Elementary?"
No one knew. So I wrote the information on the chalkboard.
"What's next?'
"Whom are we writing this letter to?" someone asked.
"Write it to a student who has the same name as you. Tell him/her what s/he might expect if s/he came to Rockdale for a day. Include how you change classes, how you go to lunch, what happens on the playground at recess, and whatever else one would experience here in one day."

They decided to boycott. No one had started to write, so I added, "You have fifteen minutes to complete your letter. I will collect them and leave them for Mr. Clement when he returns." Gradually they began the task. Before they finished, I was called to the office. An instructional assistant was sent to replace me. I explained the assignment and asked her to collect the letters and leave them on the desk for the teacher.

The next day, Mr. Clement came up to me on the playground and asked if I had read the letters the students wrote. "No. I had to leave before they finished. The Instructional Assistant left them on your desk." "You should read them. They are very revealing. I want you to; especially read what the children said about you and the principal." "Did you show them to him?" "No, I don't want to do that. He may not like them." "O.K. I'll read them." Indeed the letters were revealing! These are some of the contents:

"Don't ever come to Rockdale. If you do, and if you get into trouble, try to go to Mr. Perry. He won't do anything except fuss at you. Don't go to Mrs. Hooker; you might not like your punishment." "If you ever come to Rockdale, you won't like the lunchroom. It is so loud. The children throw food at each other." "This school is a zoo. The only principal who will discipline you is Mrs. Hooker. Try to go to Mr. Perry if you get into trouble." "Some of the teachers are good and kind, but some of them are not. And, they give hard work." "If you come here be sure you know how to fight because somebody will hit you and if you don't hit back, other students will fight you."

I thought the principal should read the comments, so I showed them to him, and asked, "What do you think of these letters written by one of Mr. Clement's gym classes?"

141

After he read a few of them, he responded, "Well, the letters show that the students like me better than they like you." "Is that all they show?"

As the letters revealed, much of the rowdiness began as the classes were dismissed for lunch. One of my duties was to monitor the lunchroom. I stationed myself to be available as the children were entering the cafeteria. A third grade boy, Sam, liked to try to jump up to dislodge the hall clock. I pulled him aside and talked with him. "Sam, you are coming to the lunchroom to eat, not to play. You may play after lunch. And, if you accidentally knock that clock down, someone will be hurt. Please don't do that again. If you do, you will not be permitted in the lunchroom." The next day, he did it again. So, I sent him directly to the playground. He began to cry. When he saw his sixth-grade brother, Sam reported that he had not been allowed to eat his lunch. His brother confronted me. "You wouldn't let my little brother eat lunch." "I warned Sam what would happen. I told him he would have to skip lunch if he continued to jump up and try to knock the hall clock down." "I'm going to beat you're ass!" "What did you say?" I pointed my finger at him for emphasis as I commanded, "Go to my office right now!"

When we reached the office, I said to him, "Call your mother." He called. When she answered he started, "This woman wouldn't let Sam eat lunch." Responding to his mother's query, he continued, "Sam was crying. He said she wouldn't let him eat lunch." I took the telephone. "Mrs. Jones, can you come to school right now?" "Who is this?" "This is Mrs. Hooker. I need to talk with you about your son." She came immediately. "Now, tell your mother again what happened." "She wouldn't let Sam eat lunch." I explained to her what Sam had done and how he had been warned what would happen if he repeated his actions. Turning to Sam's brother, I said, "Tell your mother why you were sent to the office." "I asked you why you wouldn't let my little brother eat lunch, and you sent me to the office." "What did you say to me? Did you say you would 'beat my ass'?" His mother was stunned! "You said that to the principal? I'm going to beat your ass! Go to the house right now!"

She took him home. When he came back, he was well behaved. On many occasions, it was necessary to show consistency with the children, and sometimes with their parents. One Christmas, we had visitors for an assembly. By way of introduction, I said to the children,

"Let's show our guests how appreciative students at Rockdale can be. Please remove your chewing gum and sit up straight in your seats." A fifth-grader looked right at me, opened her purse, took out a stick of gum, and put it in her mouth.

On my way out the door, I whispered to her, 'Go to my office right now!" When we arrived there, I asked her "Why were you sent to the office?" "When you said 'Take your gum out' I put some in my mouth." "That is called willful defiance. For your action, you will not be allowed to go with your class on the next field trip. Call your mother." When her mother answered the phone the girl began to cry, saying that Mrs. Hooker said she could not go with the class for the next field trip. Her mother said she would be at the school shortly.

Meanwhile, I wrote a notice explaining why Grace could not go with her class. I handed the note to her mother as she entered the office. The girl began to cry uncontrollably. She went into the hallway, paced the floor in a circle, and caused a loud disturbance. Teachers came into the hallway to see what was happening. The mother snatched the note from my hand and began tearing it up, saying, "That's what I think of your note!" Then she began to tell me what she thought of black folks when they get a little authority. I rang the buzzer under my desk, and started to leave the office. The secretary came to the door in response to the buzzer. I told her, "Please call District Four." Now the mother really became emotional. The daughter was bellowing and the mother was yelling.

When the police arrived, I asked them not to leave unless they took the mother with them. When one of the policemen asked her to come with him, she said, "I don't want any of my children here!" The secretary asked me what she should do. "Call the other child and tell her to bring all of her things with her. Then write the transfers for the children."

The younger daughter came downstairs. When she saw her mother and sister, she thought something tragic had happened. Her mother told her that they would be leaving Rockdale for good. The mother and her daughters left with the policeman.

The next day was the last day before winter break. After the winter break, the dad, a Marine, came to the school to talk with me. "My wife doesn't mean half of what she says. She's hot-tempered." I explained to him what had happened. He said he understood but he wanted to know if he could bring his daughters back to school. I told him his wife had withdrawn them and she would have to reinstate them. "I know she took them out. But she can't enroll them in North Avondale or South Avondale unless she has a valid reason for withdrawing them from Rockdale. " "I knew that, but there was no way to tell her because she was in no mood to listen." "Then may I bring them back?" "No. She took them out and she should bring them back. Your wife needs to know how her negative behavior affects her children."

When she brought them back she was so subdued she was hardly recognizable. I explained to her that the teachers were under no obligation to allow her daughters to make up their missed work, but they could do so if they chose. That solved the problem with the mother, but the principal was angry that I had called the police. "Mrs. Hooker, do you realize that I have been here fourteen years and I have never called the police?" My response was, "Why?"

Word gets around. The Director of Personnel came to see me at Rockdale. I had written a letter to him protesting my principal's demeaning behavior toward me. Dr. Orebaugh laughed and slapped his leg as he said, "Word gets around, doesn't it? I don't think you will have trouble with any more parents challenging you."

Dr. Orebaugh offered to transfer me to another school, if I wanted to do so. But I really wanted to continue to help the children and the teachers at Rockdale. By now I knew that my presence was beginning to be appreciated by some of the teachers, some of the parents, and many of the students.

For the 1984-85 school year, I was assigned to Rockdale and Washburn Elementary. I spent two days at one school and three at the other for one week, then vice versa the next week. The principal at Washburn had discipline under control – for the students and the teachers. She personally visited each classroom each day, even though there were three floors in the building. The principal and I shared lunchroom and playground duties. However, we divided the workload for teacher evaluations.

One of the teachers I had to evaluate had taught third grade for more than twenty-five years. I wondered why she needed to be evaluated. When I observed in her classroom, I knew why. The children were completely out of control. And, of course, they were learning that their misbehavior was being rewarded. When the teacher and I had our follow-up conference, I told her what I had observed, and asked her to verify or differ with my observations. She agreed that she allowed them to do what they wanted; because that way she had no problems with them.

"But you are hired to teach them," I reminded her.
"Well you can't teach them if they don't want to learn."
I asked the principal to give me some information about the teacher. It was confirmed that her class tested the lowest in the school.

"Then why hasn't she been removed?"
"Odessa, do you know it costs nearly $40,000 to get rid of a teacher?"
"What about the children? Her damage to them in incalculable."
I was left to handle the matter as I saw fit. I called the teacher's union and asked them to evaluate her performance. The union personnel assigned to observe her wanted my opinion. I declined to give it. "You are qualified to evaluate her; I expect you to do so." Even the union admitted that she was unqualified. She was dismissed. But I was angry. I said to the principal, "This kind of thing is only allowed to happen in schools with predominantly black children!"

I used the same tactic to have an incompetent teacher dismissed at Rockdale. The good teachers received my support to become even better.

My next assignment was Rockdale and Westwood Elementary. The principal at Rockdale gave me assignments that were not well thought out. For example, he requested I do the scheduling for the standardized testing at Rockdale, knowing that I would not be present for some of the test days. Nevertheless, I made a detailed schedule and presented it to the staff the week before the testing started. I met with them and asked them to examine the schedule and see if any changes needed to be made. I also met with the instructional assistants to go over the schedule with them. They too understood it. Everyone understood the schedule.

The first day of testing at Rockdale, I was at Westwood. Two or three teachers from Rockdale called to ask for clarification about the testing schedule.

"Are you following the schedule?"

"Well last year we didn't do it like this."

"I'm sorry but I am not scheduled to return to Rockdale until the day after tomorrow. You will have to figure it out for yourselves."

When I returned to Rockdale, one of the instructional assistants said, "Mrs. Hooker, your schedule was perfect. Some of the teachers decided they wanted to change it to suit their convenience." "Thank you." I spoke to the Rockdale principal about his teachers calling me at Westwood. The principal said, "The scheduling was your responsibility, so when they came to me, I told them to call you."

At Westwood, the experience was different. The student population was predominantly white. The principal did not concern herself with anything unpleasant. Some days she would hide in her office. I received mixed reviews from the parents. I was accused of being prejudiced by both white and black parents. I chose to ignore that. My first challenge was a parent who worried the principal and the teachers incessantly. Her son was her life. When I arrived at the school, Danny was in fourth grade.

One day the principal said to me, "Will you talk to Danny's mother?" The mother complained about how some children teased her son. She walked this child to school every morning, and returned to walk him home every afternoon. His lunch was packed because he was allergic to certain foods. I observed him on the playground and in the lunchroom. He was frail and didn't interact very well with the other children, but I saw nothing that required my interference. Almost daily, the mother wanted to tell me something that one of the children had said to or about Danny.

After listening to her patiently for several meetings, I said, "Mrs. Clark, each of us is given different gifts. Danny is your gift. He has to learn to get along with others. You can help him by encouraging him not to tattle to you about everything that happens. If he has a serious concern, he should be encouraged to bring it to our attention; otherwise, we need to allow Danny to learn to deal with his own problems." She lessened the frequency of her complaints, but when it was time to send Danny to a different school, she started again. "Danny isn't ready to go to another school. He really needs to stay at Westwood. Don't you think he is too young to go to junior high school?" She was unsuccessful. Danny was promoted.

I also received a promotion - to Roselawn Condon, a school for orthopedically handicapped, multi-handicapped children, which also included a non-handicapped component. It was a fascinating assignment. The grade levels ranged from kindergarten through eighth grade. The multi-handicapped children were mainstreamed for many of their subjects; for others, there were special teachers. There were physical therapists, occupational therapists, speech therapists, a psychologist, and a school nurse on staff. There was also a home economics teacher for the multi-handicapped students. The building was on one level, with wide doorways and hallways to accommodate wheel chairs. Special helpers accompanied some of the students.

The most remarkable aspect of the school was the way the students related to each other. The non-handicapped students felt privileged to push a wheel chair. They had to be restrained from having wheel chair races or activities that were dangerous. All the students went to the lunchroom together. Some of the multi-handicapped children could eat independently.

Because of my certification, I worked primarily with the elementary classes. This was my first assignment with a single school. Several buses came to the school every day. Some of the severely handicapped children came in a bus alone. One of the major responsibilities I had was bus duty; I had to be present for the arrival and the departure of the buses.

If children are expected to obey rules, they should know the rules. Therefore, on the first day of school, an assembly was called for bus riders. I talked about the importance and the responsibility of being a bus rider. "We provide you with a bus ride because we want you to arrive at school safely. If you are on the bus, you will not run into dogs or other harmful circumstances. You do not have to walk in the rain or other inclement weather. We ask you to help us by following these rules:
- Keep your body inside the bus at all times.
- Remain in your assigned seat.
- Talk with a soft voice
- Keep your hands to yourself.

If you obey these rules, the bus driver can concentrate on his/her job, and will not be distracted. The driver is not expected to have to stop the bus to get your cooperation. If the driver writes you up for distracting him/her, I will remind you one time. If there is a second write-up, I will talk with your parents. If there is a third write-up, you will lose your privilege to ride the bus." Then I distributed the printed Regulations for Bus Riders. "Please go over these rules with your parents. Ask them to sign them and send them back tomorrow. I will collect them as you get off the bus."

In my tenure at Roselawn Condon, it was necessary to suspend only two students from the bus. One boy was warned about fighting. On his third write-up, I took him off the bus that day. I drove him home and informed his mother that he would have to find another way to get to school. She protested, but she had to drive him to school for the remainder of the year.

The following is an incident that involved a parent's disagreement with me; it happened toward the end of the school year at Roselawn Condon. The music teacher rehearsed after school daily to prepare the performers for the school graduation day program. I was returning to my office after bus duty. A boy walked past me with his hat on. I knew the principal's rule about boys wearing hats in the building, but it was the end of the day, school was out, so I ignored him. He wanted to make sure I noticed him, so he walked back in front of me, turned around, walked toward me again, and pulled the bib of his cap to the side of his head to call my attention to it. As I walked past him, I reached up, took the cap off his head, and went into my office. He came behind me saying, "You better give me back my hat!"

I went to the music room to find out why he was not in rehearsal. The music teacher said that she had not excused him to leave the room. With her permission, I excluded him from participation in the final program.

The next day his mother came in to talk about what had happened. I told her about the incident, concluding, "In fact, not satisfied that I had not noticed him, he deliberately called himself to my attention. Mrs. Thomas assured me that he had caused enough problems to be excluded from the band." The mother threatened to call the board of education. Instead, she called the principal. He asked me what had happened, and when I explained the incident, he agreed with my actions. Later, the dad called. I would not reverse my ruling. Both parents were angry. The next year they took their son out of public school.

148

I met them again when their son became a FISC scholar at one of the FISC schools. They were so surprised to meet me. The father said, "We didn't know you were the coordinator of the FISC Scholars program!" I said nothing about the incident. Four years later, I was pleased to note that he graduated from college and now works as an engineer.

As an administrator, consistency was my most valuable tool in maintaining discipline. I insisted that the children always be taught the rules and the consequences for breaking them. Whenever a rule was violated, I saw to it that the child could tell me what rule had been broken, and the consequence.

Chapter 37

1990: RETIREMENT, JOB CHANGE, and SOARING FULFILLMENT

In 1990, after 31 years as a teacher and administrator, I retired. The teachers at Roselawn Condon organized a wonderful surprise retirement reception and dinner. David, Melanie, her husband, and Pearline attended.

Following retirement I was wondering how to pay Darrell's tuition at Tuskegee University.

Shortly before retiring, I had received a telephone call from the courts about Randy's child support arrearage. He was in arrears in his payments to the amount of $65, 000. Did I want to pursue this matter?

I answered, "No, thank you. The children are all grownup now. I will not upset myself by re-opening those wounds."

I did hire a lawyer, though and offered Randy the option of signing a quit claim deed or paying the arrearage. He signed the quit claim deed. He had stopped paying child support when he moved to another job out of state in 1976. I didn't have the money to pursue him in court in another state. So, I left it up to God to bring justice to the whole matter. The payments had stopped coming when Darrell was in his second year at Springer, and David was at Morehouse. I was paid twice per month. Most of one check went to Morehouse College and most of the other one went to Springer School. At that time, I said, "Well, Lord, I guess this is the year we won't eat." But when I calculated my income taxes, we had had no emergencies, no illnesses and all the bills were paid in a timely manner. I marvel at God's goodness!

In the period of launching my children, I had three of them in school at the same time: David, Melanie, and Darrell. I can't tell you how we did it because I don't know. I do know that God keeps his promises and He answers prayers.

Now, six months after retirement, my prayers for Darell's tuition were answered

150

I was hired to coordinate a minority scholarship program for a group called FISC, the Fund for Independent Schools of Cincinnati, Inc. The president of the group from 1984 through 1990 had been Clement L. Buenger. He was also president and CEO of $5^{th}/3^{rd}$ Bank in Cincinnati. In 1985, he had been reading The Cincinnati Enquirer when he observed that of the 150+ valedictorians in the Greater Cincinnati area, only three were African Americans. He surmised that Cincinnati was losing its African American leadership pool. When he articulated his concerns to the corporate community, they raised more than $2 million to establish an endowment. The purpose was to award scholarships to send African American students to independent college preparatory high schools in Cincinnati. Attendance and successful completion at these schools would guarantee their eligibility to enter college. I discovered that there were seven of these schools. I was hired to coordinate the program. The funds are given to those schools, asking them in turn to prepare African American students for leadership. There is no obligation on the part of the students, but it is hoped that some of them will return to Cincinnati to join the leadership pool. I was hired to track their progress from ninth grade through college and report to the board their career choices, and especially how many of them eventually return to Cincinnati. In my January 2003 report to the board, I shared these statistics:

In fifteen years (1988-2003) this is the record:

- 286 FISC Scholars have entered FISC high schools

- 216 have graduated from FISC high schools

- 214 have entered college; four entered the military, and one joined the National Americorps

- 104 have completed college

- 81 are still in college; 23 pursuing advanced degrees

- 70 are still in high school

- 44 are living and working in Cincinnati

I also reported that FISC may now claim its first two doctors: one M.D. and a Ph.D.

151

This work has been so satisfying. And, God is still blessing me. After paying the last tuition, I started a fund for African American Independent Christian Schools. The idea grew out of another assignment I accepted, from a group called the Cincinnati chapter of the Amistad Research Center. At one of the group's meetings, I suggested they recognize educators who have opened schools for African American children. It was my idea, so I was given the assignment. My research uncovered more than ten independent academies for African American children in Cincinnati. Churches operated most of them; none of them included twelve grades. And none of them had computer laboratories. So, with no more obligation to pay tuition, I started the fund to benefit these schools. It is managed by The Greater Cincinnati Foundation.

In 1993, a neighbor nominated me to become an Enquirer Woman of the Year. This honor is given to ten women in Cincinnati each year. The Cincinnati Enquirer, the leading local newspaper in the city, sponsors the program. The purpose is to recognize women volunteers in Cincinnati who have made a difference. Community letters to The Enquirer are used to select the nominees. In 1993, 504 letters were sent and 87 women were nominated. I came in first. Pat Collins, a friend and neighbor nominated me. She also worked to solicit support from my family and other people who knew me. Receiving the award was quite an honor. Subsequently, Pat and I organized the Wess Park Drive Prayer Group, which is still in operation. We meet the second and fourth Wednesdays of the month in our homes – alternating the hosting among members.

The Cincinnati Enquirer Woman of the year recognition was the first of many more such honors. In 1998, I was the recipient of three awards:

- The Lighthouse Youth Services Beacon of Light Humanitarian Award was given in recognition of the work of Summerbridge Cincinnati, Inc. I co-founded this education workshop in 1992 with the help of William H. Hopple, Jr. We celebrated ten years of this successful program in September 2002.

- The National Council of Women, Cincinnati Section, gave to me the Bethune Recognition Award for volunteer service.

152

- The Delta Sigma Theta Sorority, Inc of Cincinnati presented to me an award for Community Services.

- In 1999 Summerbridge Cincinnati, Inc. was awarded the *APPLAUSE!* Magazine Award for service to education.

- In 2000, I was one of five recipients to receive the Otto Armleder Award for service to the community.

While attending St. Peter's United Church of Christ in Cincinnati, the pastor nominated me to receive the EXCELLENCE in TEACHING Award, which is granted to five people in the country. I was one of those who were presented this honor on July 14, 2001 at the United Church of Christ General Synod in Kansas City, Missouri.

In that same year, I also received one other recognition. The Women's Fund of The Greater Cincinnati Foundation published a book which profiles the contributions of several women who make a difference in the lives of those around them. I am one of thirty women profiled in *LIFE LESSONS AT HER TABLE.*

Chapter 38

1998 – 1999: DEATH of PARENTS

One day in 1985 I received a call from my dad; he announced that Mama was sick. When I spoke with her, her voice was almost unrecognizable. It was gruff and slurred. Her response to my inquiry about her health was that she didn't feel well. "What's hurting you, Mama?" "I don't know, Odessa; I just feel sick." Daddy came back to the telephone. "Dessa Ree, all she says is, 'I'm sick'." "Did you take her to the doctor yet?" "No, I don't know how to tell him what's ailing her." "Daddy, I think she shouldn't be left alone." See if you can get someone to stay with her until you can get an appointment to take her to the doctor."

For the next thirteen years, we took Mama to many doctors – in Cincinnati, in Los Angeles and in Florida where different siblings wanted their doctor to examine her. In addition to an operation to remove her gall bladder, she was finally diagnosed as being clinically depressed. We went back and forth with treatments designed to improve her condition. Nothing worked.

The strain on Daddy was severe; he began to show signs of breaking. So, Pearline and I began to drive thirteen hours one way back and forth to Moultrie, every time we got a four-day holiday break from work. Daddy was grateful for the relief. Her condition worsened to the point where we had to arrange to place her in a nursing home. Daddy visited every day, practically all day.

But he was uncomfortable leaving her in the nursing home, so he requested her release. Again he tried to care for her at home. Finally, he himself became ill. He reported that he was so exhausted or so mentally foggy, that he fell asleep at the wheel of his taxicab. We hired help to be with Mama seven hours per day. The aide assisted Mama with her morning bath and dress. She also cooked their meals, and served them lunch. Then Daddy would serve the dinner she left prepared, and clean the kitchen.

However, the strain became too much after he had prostate surgery. While he was recovering, a brother and sister who lived in Moultrie took turns helping and staying with them at night. Daddy had been experiencing something he called 'sick spells'. These were slight heart attacks. He was wearing a pacemaker. One night, he had another 'sick spell.' To avoid waking Mama, he crawled out of bed and went into another room to call my sister who lived in Moultrie. When she arrived, he asked for more pillows to prop himself up. Then he asked for covers; he felt cold. She called my brother to come and take him to the hospital. He died before getting to the hospital.

Daddy died December 29, 1997; we buried him January 3, 1998. My dad's death deeply affected all of us. He had been a rock of strength for us all. He left us a powerful legacy. My sister Betty felt some guilt because she and Freddie had promised to care for Daddy and Mama, instead of having Pearline and me try to do so from a distance. She felt she should have been with him the night he died, but instead she was at her home. Nevertheless, we came together to make funeral arrangements and to decide what to do about Mama. All the siblings except the Jehovah's Witnesses in our family attended Daddy's funeral. Many people in Moultrie also attended the funeral. Those who knew Daddy, as well as those who had benefited from his many kindnesses came to show their last respects. Darrell composed a poem to Granddaddy. He titled it "Monday Crickets." I sang a solo at the funeral.

My oldest brother, Anderson Jr. was named the executor of the estate. He asked, "Mama, what do you want to do?" She replied, "Anderson, Jr. your daddy told me that you all would take care of me."

And we did. Pearline and I are the oldest, and the ones who had retired. We took the lead in caring for Mama. We took turns spending two weeks each with her. I traveled back and forth by bus to and from Atlanta, Georgia. Each of my three sons took turns meeting me at the bus station and driving me to Moultrie – about three and one half-hours. We began to make arrangements to bring Mama to Cincinnati. Our youngest sister, Andrea was to return to Cincinnati and purchase a house that would accommodate Mama – no stairs. Pearline and I also took care of preparing our parent's house for sale or lease. We offered all the siblings whatever furnishings they wanted to keep. We had a yard sale to get rid of the rest. With the proceeds, we had the house repaired and painted before selling or leasing it. Daddy's car went to Betty.

After my two-week stay with Mama, Pearline was to relieve me so I could return to Cincinnati. Prior to Dad's death I had agreed to sing at a Learning Links presentation at The Greater Cincinnati Foundation. Daddy's death was fresh on my mind, so I sang two songs that represented two life-long lessons my dad had taught us: (1) anything worth doing is worth praying about; and (2) after you pray, remember to say 'Thank you.' The songs I sang were *The Lord's Prayer* and *My Tribute,* by Andre Crouch.

Meanwhile, Andrea had purchased a home, and we made arrangements to fly Mama to Cincinnati. Pearline was to fly with her, and Andrea and I would take care meeting her in Cincinnati to take her to her new home. On the Sunday before the planned departure, and just before my return to Moultrie to help Pearline with final arrangements, she called to tell me that Mama had fallen and had broken her hip. She was operated on the next day; but died a few hours later.

Mama and Daddy were buried just seventy days apart. Once again the family gathered to mourn the loss of our parents. I sang at her funeral. After the service, we all agreed that we knew she wanted to join Daddy. They had been married sixty-eight years and had never been apart for more than two weeks during their marriage. We never expected one to live very long after the other died. I was relieved that they were together again.

As we gathered in the house, we began to swap stories about Mama and Daddy. I recalled Daddy's faithful work in the church. He was a life-long member of Union Baptist Church. He served in many offices. These statistics are recorded in the church records:

> President of the Senior Choir, Oct. 26, 1951 – 1967
> Teacher of Men's Sunday school class. 1953 – later stages of illness
> Deacon, May 8, 1959 – until death
> Church treasurer, Nov. 20, 1959 – 1989
> Chairman, 1989 – 1993
> He also organized the weekly prayer meeting, 1967

At his funeral, one of the deacons remarked, "Deacon Walker was a faithful member of this church all his life. You could count on him to be a positive contributor in whatever way he could. I remember when we decided to build a new church. Many people doubted that we could do so, but Deacon Walker believed that with God's help we could do it. Members were asked to make a pledge to the new building. Deacon Walker pledged $10,000 for himself and $5,000 for Mrs. Walker. And, true to his word, he kept his promise. Even through Mrs. Walker's illness, he paid his tithes and his pledge. When we counted the contributions, Deacon Walker had paid more than his pledge. That's the kind of man he was. He always walked with his head held high."

I recalled how he used to sing:
"I got to live the life I sing about in my soul.
I got to do the best I can, love and serve my fellowman,
I got to live the life I sing about in my soul."

His signature song was
I Can Put My Trust In Jesus; Can He put His Trust In Me:
There are those who will deceive me, no matter how my trust may be
Even friends and nearest kindred sometimes turn their backs on me;
But there is One who always listens, and my poor condition sees –
I can put my trust in Jesus, can He put His trust in me?
Do I help those who are needy, just like Jesus has helped me?
Do I give my best in service, even though no one can see?
I can say He is my Savior, and from sin He set me free-
I can put my trust in Jesus. can He put His trust in me?

Pearline told of a woman who called the house a few days after Daddy's death. Pearline didn't remember her name, but the woman wanted to offer a few words of comfort to us. She told of how her family was so grateful to Dad for being there for them. "As a busy cab driver, trying to make a living, Mr. Walker was always willing to help when other people needed assistance. I am a hard-working single parent with three children. One time the doctor said I had to have surgery; I would need to be in the hospital for a week. I got special permission for my children to come and visit me while I was in the hospital. I paid Mr. Walker to bring the girls to visit every day. He would bring them, then wait to take them back home.
"I was surprised and disappointed when the doctor said I had to stay another week. I had budgeted for only one week. When Mr. Walker heard about it, he told me not to worry about the money; he would continue to 'haul' the girls back and forth. That second week the weather turned cool. Mr. Walker was kind enough to build a fire in the fireplace for the girls when he took them home.

"Honey, your dad was truly a generous, Christian man. They don't come like him anymore. We will always remember him."

I realized that I had never heard some of these stories. I became interested in how some of my brothers and sisters saw my parents. I wanted to learn more about their legacy and our family history. I wanted to tell how my poor parents entered this world with nothing, and left it debt free and a better place to live.

The Hooker Children 1963
Left to right
Darrell (inset) 6 mos. Sept. 16, 1969
Margaret - 3 yrs. Dec. 14, 1960
David - 5 yrs. Oct. 15, 1958
Melanie - 6 yrs. Aug. 22, 1957
Douglas - 9 yrs. March 31, 1954

Melanie (11) and Margaret (8) slide down
posts supporting basketball hoop

David plays with his dog , Sport
1968

In 1988, the family looked like this:

Top row left to right: Douglas Hooker, Arthur Johnson, Odessa (mother),
Margert Houlton (bride) Homer(father of bride) Darrell , & David.
Center row, left to right: Patrise (Douglas's wife) Melanie (Arthur's wife)
Bottom row : Douglas Patrick & Randi Michelle Hooker.

The Hooker Clan
ont row: Douglas, Patrise, Lael
ck row: Randi Michelle, Letia,
Douglas Patrick
2001

Darrell W. & LaTonya Hooker
Wedding 1996
Darrell McKenna (inset)
13 months

Douglas Patrick Hooker
Letia Hill Hooker
and
Lael Darice Hooker

mer Randolph Hooker and Odessa
casion: Honeymoon January 1953

Odessa, an Enquirer Woman
of the Year.
1994

Odessa poses with FISC scholars after accepting the
Applause! Magazine Award; given to Summerbridge Cincinnati: 1999
scholars: Gabriel & Frenika Mudd, Andrea Merrick & Rahwa Ghebre-Ab

Odessa and other recipients
of Otto Armleder Award
November 2000

Odessa and other recipients the Teaching in "Excellence Award"
given by the United Church of Christ- Kansas City, Kansas
2001

Pearline and Odessa as they appeared in Life Lessons
at Her Table: The stories of women who make a difference in the lives of those around them.
2001

Part Three

Chapter 39

HOW OTHER FAMILY MEMBERS REMEMBERED

MAMA and DADDY

When the idea of writing these memoirs came to me, I shared with other family members what I wanted to do. I wrote them a letter, saying "I have recorded Mama's and Daddy's story as I remembered it. Now, would each of you submit to me your own recollections of them?" Some of the family responded. There were also responses from some other people. I would like to share the same as I received them.

Second oldest child, Pearline, stated:

I admired the pride Mom showed in keeping the house clean. Each one of us had daily chores to do. However, there were some chores that hindered my breathing and caused me to sneeze. I seemed to stay sick a lot; had pneumonia three times before I got to school. She decided to rescue me from all the sweeping and dusting chores. My new assigned chores included helping in the kitchen. That's when I learned to cook. I enjoyed making Banana puddings so much that it became our standard Sunday dessert.

Another memory of Mom's compassionate nature included her taking care of Dad's sick relatives. It was in the early forties when Dad went and brought Granddaddy Jim, (Dad's father) to our house. Granddaddy had suffered a stroke; he couldn't talk or walk. Dad had built a small room next to our house and placed his father in it. Each day Mom would feed and take care of him. One day I got the chance to feed him and I will never forget the sad look in his eyes. I really didn't know him very well because he wasn't around very much as we grew up. All I remember is that he left Grandmama Carrie and the three children and never came back. Years later, after Granddaddy died, Aunt Maggie got sick and came to live with us. When Aunt Maggie died, then Grandmama Carrie came and lived with us. When she became ill, Mom took care of her until she died also. When I look back over these years I realize that Mom had been 'over worked', as the old folks would say. I'm sure Mom's servant role did not go

167

unnoticed by God, for in His Word Jesus states, "Whoever wants to become great among you must be your servant." (Mark 10:43 NIV). And Luke notes, "Your care of others is the measure of your greatness." (10:48b TLB). I remember hearing Gramdmama Carrie say, "If anybody's going to heaven, it's gonna be Pauline." Mom's faith in God helped her to be there for both families. I, too, believe she's in heaven now and I thank God for allowing her to leave such a great legacy of compassion and love for us to emulate.

It was 1952, my junior year at Florida A&M University, when I had a leading role in the Playmakers Guild's Spring Production. We took the play to my hometown, Moultrie, which was only sixty-four miles north of Tallahassee. On the day before the trip I remembered to ask Mom to fix a few refreshments for the cast; it would be served when the play was over. We only lived a few houses down from the high school where the production was to take place.

There was so much excitement around our small town, and everything was set in place for our touring group. The auditorium was packed. Dad had found a front seat for my other family members – except Mom, who was at home getting things ready for the reception. The play was successful and was the talk of the town for a long, long time. In fact, someone mentioned it to me at our 50th high school class reunion in1999.

When we arrived for the reception, Mom had prepared every kind of food you could think of, including fried chicken and potato salad. Everything was so festive and delicious! You can imagine how proud I was when the entire group kept pouring on the compliments to Mom. She was tired but delighted that everyone had an enjoyable time. I did not realize all the hard work and sacrifice Mom must have experienced in preparation for us. Sometime later, she expressed a desire to have seen the play – I had had a big role and she had never seen me act before. I can truly say that she was always there for us. What a blessing! Due to time and space constraints I can not share all the many times we had together. But I am so thankful to God for her kind-hearted, unselfish and giving spirit. She will always have a special place in my heart.

I always felt that Dad was a great problem-solver. He was a hard worker who always managed more than one job. This meant that we didn't get to see much of him during the week. So we wrote notes asking for money for school needs, then placed them on the mantel over the fireplace before going to bed. We couldn't stay up to wait for Dad to get home from work, and he'd be gone by the time we got up the next morning. We could trust him to leave the money on top of each note. I remember once when Dess wrote a note requesting a sum much larger than usual. I went to bed thinking about it. Dess and I shared a bed, so when she had fallen asleep that night, I sneaked out of bed and placed my note on top of hers. This would assure me that my request was granted *first* before the money ran out (smile). Needless to say, Daddy always solved our money problems and our needs were fully met.

One of the most memorable recollections of Dad happened when he was faced with sending Dess to college. He shared this story with us much later. Dad worked for Swift's Meatpacking Company for years; he watched many of his co-workers go to the credit office to borrow money to buy a new car. The highest amount one could borrow was $500.00. So on this day when Daddy went to the credit office and requested a loan for $1000.00, the loan officer was shocked. (This was in 1947, in Small Town, USA, and Daddy was a Black man.) The loan officer thought Daddy wanted to buy a car. He was shocked again when Daddy told him that he needed the money to send his daughter to college. The loan officer shared Dad's story with the supervisor. The supervisor was so impressed that the money was granted with an invitation to get more when needed. Praise the Lord! God had opened another door for Dad. "We have not because we ask not." James 4:2 Pastor Charles Stanley wrote, "The way we respond to the trials of life reveals the level of our faith." I saw Dad step out on faith many times. He and Mom were married at a very young age, but they knew how to call on God for help. This saw them through the hard times and sustained them through their long 68-year marriage. They were far from perfect; sometimes they made poor choices, but thank God there were better good than bad choices. We never doubted their love for us. We were poor and didn't know it. We were truly blessed to have been born into such a wonderful loving and God-fearing family.

Pearline Walker R. Singletary, Retired educator

Fourth sibling, first son, Anderson Walker, Jr.

Some things I remember about Mom. At the age of four or five, somewhere in there, I remember Mom taking me to the grocery store, showing me how to pick out things and put them in a shopping cart. It didn't seem important then but I know now how important it is. When we got to the checkout counter, someone would be rude to Mom. I'd ask her about it. She said, "Junior, don't worry about it." I also remember Mom taught me how to make mud pies. To me that was a big thing. I was a little kid and it was important to me to know how to do something, and I could make money. I knew the meter reader would come by and buy those mud pies from me. I thought that was great. Most important of all, Mama would take me to church. I remember I asked a lot of questions. At the age of eight I told Mama I was ready to be baptized. I never realized how important that was until I became older and wiser – knowing the things of life and spiritual things Mom taught me.

Some of the things I remember about Dad. I recall when I was four years of age Dad took me fishing. I didn't know anything about fishing but I guess because I was a little boy, Dad wanted to teach me to fish. I was wearing short pants. He took me down to the creek and the yellow flies would bite me. I would slap the flies. Dad said, "Junior, you're making noise and you'll scare the fish away."

Being obedient, I stopped slapping the flies; I would just brush them off. After being down there for a couple of hours or so, I had red marks all over me where I had been bitten by the yellow flies. Mama told Dad, "Don't take my baby down there any more." That was comical to me later on.

Dad would also take me to Tallahassee to see Pearline in school. He'd say, "Junior, take this money to your sister." Dad took me many places. He called me 'Sport Model.' I don't know where that came from but he'd say, "See my little Sport."

I realize now that he took as much time with me as he could, but I always wondered why he was never around to watch me play ball or do anything like that. When I was much older I realized that with nine children, he didn't have much time to do anything except provide for his family. Those are some of the things I remember about Dad. He

170

had a strong will and determination to educate his children. It fills my heart with joy when I remember how I watched my dad go from one job to another. He'd come home from Swift's Meatpacking Co. and go right out again. He was headed for Mr. Felton's Dry Cleaners to deliver clothes. Dad always did SOMETHING! It seems he always wanted to own something – a business of his own.

That dream came true in 1964. After he retired from Swift's Meatpacking Co., he started his own taxicab business. I guess that's what's inside me. I always want to own something or have something. I know I got that from my Dad.

Anderson Walker, Jr. Retired Amtrak Ticket Agent

Sixth born and fourth sister, Oreatha Walker Ensley

Mom: Scenario: High school year (eleventh or twelfth grade). I came home from some event or activity - I really don't remember the details, but I thought Mom and Dad were asleep. I was not sneaking, just trying to be quiet.

Mom called from the back room, "Oreatha, don't you think it's a little late to be coming in?"

She said nothing else, but I remembered that the next time, and I made sure to come in much earlier. I knew that in order for her to trust me, I needed to show that I was responsible. That was a lesson learned by trial and error. She did not choose to punish or whip me.

Mom loved to get her feet massaged and toe nails clipped. We would sit around in the living room talking while I took care of her feet. She always taught us discipline and focus. We could not leave the house until the beds were made, the dishes washed, etc. This was the rule even on school days. The house stayed clean and spotless. Everyone had some chore, depending on our age.

I remember when Mom would make me go out and get my own switch. She sure knew how to make us think about what we had done.

I loved her laugh. She would double over sometimes without warning, laughing at some of the things we did.

I will never forget this incident. It happened my first year at Talladega University; I had worked that summer to buy winter clothes. I knew that I would have to go back home to switch my summer clothes for my winter clothes. I had bought this beautiful black and white speckled coat with a large collar that came up around my ears. I got home to pack my clothes, but could not find my coat. Mom had given it to someone she thought really needed it! She told me she never saw me wear it; therefore, she gave it to someone less fortunate. I cried. But even now I will do the same thing: if I have not used some item of clothing for a year, I will give it to charity.

Dad always worked – one job, two jobs – however many it took to take care of us. I remember Dad teaching me to count all the coins he had. He would put them on the bed, then have us separate them into denominations. We would count each group, then Dad would show us how to add them all together. He was a genius when it came to money and business.

Every day, when he got home from work he would drive up into the yard – slowly while we jumped on the running board of the Mercury. That was a lot of fun.

Dad taught me that there was always a way to solve a problem. I also loved sitting in the living room with Dad shelling peanuts and popping them into my mouth with a steady rhythm. He loved nuts.

One thing he did that I didn't like was to compare me with Ellen Everett. I don't care how hard I tried or how well I did, it was not as good as Ellen. I got over that eventually. He meant well; he just didn't realize that it didn't help my self-esteem.

Dad and Mom taught me that good hard work never hurt anyone; it just made me more determined to do the best job I could. Never give up. Get your education. Neither of them finished high school, but they wanted us to do so. I really learned to love and appreciate both of them, especially when I had my own family.

Oreatha L. Walker Ensley, Retired educator

Oreatha's husband, Mose, also sent comments.

I remember Mama and Daddy. I think I first have to mention the calmness and gentleness of Mama. Oreatha used to tell me how she never raised her voice but could always get her point across – with a stare or a shoe thrown across the room in her direction. I can remember how she handled things in her life. Whether we were talking about a crisis in the world, our family, or just talking about things in general, she always approached things from the reality "it could be worse."

I remember Mama came to Los Angeles to be with Oreatha and the family before Letitia was born. I don't know if she realized how much that meant to us as a family. It was going to be a new experience for Oreatha and it was very special having her mother close by her side. This gave me a great sense of comfort also. I realized her life had always been one of willing to give and share.

When Mama was ill and came to Los Angeles for medical care, she spent one month with us. We had a chance to share many things. Many of them were personal. Many early mornings, after playing one of my music jobs, we would sit in the open door of my van and talk for hours. Some of the experiences she shared with me will always be special. Long before we had those talks, I mentioned to Oreatha many times that Mama is a lady way ahead of her times. She had a special mission to raise a family and be a friend to many. She was a lady who really understood many things that many people didn't. She surprised me at times. Eventually I understood that you could talk to her about anything; she was one of God's gifts to her children, to those who loved her and to the universe. Her sweet soft personality, gentle smile, and love will always be a part of my life and our children's. She is missed but not forgotten; her presence is always felt.

How do you start off talking about Daddy without mentioning that great big smile and laugh of his. He had such a generous laugh. When he laughed with you or at you, he could make you feel you were the most important person on earth. He was always a great talker and listener. I will never forget watching him as he took care of his taxi service, his church activities, and his other chores. And how he would talk to and play with his grandchildren!

I will always remember the special time he and I had together when he came to California because Mama was ill – the times we talked about her and how he cried when he talked about Mama. We went to Universal Studios and many other places together while he was here. It was wonderful to see how much he really enjoyed himself. I remember especially how he laughed when we had dinner at Benihana's Restaurant. He would just roll when the cook flipped the food up in the air and caught it. We have wonderful pictures of those moments that I will always cherish.

Now the fishing – a man after my own heart. I couldn't help but like a man who loved to fish. And Daddy loved fishing! I remember one year during a family reunion in Moultrie, I woke up looking for Daddy; he had left and gone fishing to catch fish for the fish fry that evening. He said he thought we needed just a little more fish to add to the fish that he had caught earlier that week. Sure enough, he came back with more fish; we had a grand fish fry that afternoon.

I remember how we would be eager to receive the pecans Daddy and Mama sent each year. I remember the picture of him serving as deacon in the church and leading the congregation in song. He loved his church. He, too, had a big heart and was not afraid to share his life with his family and with others. Daddy, like Mama will always be a part of my life and I am thankful for both of them. I am a better person for having shared just a small part of my life with them.

> Daddy's and Mama's loving son-in-law, Mose M. Ensley, Jr., Retired, Senior Manufacturing Coordinator, Electronics (Aerospace), McDonnell Douglas Corp.

Andrea, seventh born, fifth daughter

I remember Mother's generous spirit. I had worked all summer in Deal, NJ, and had bought winter clothes and a large trunk to leave them in until I returned home at Thanksgiving; at that time I would exchange the summer clothes for the winter ones. I had locked the trunk and left the key with Mother for safekeeping. When I returned home for Thanksgiving, I immediately went to the trunk to exchange the clothes. NOTHING! Absolutely nothing was found in the trunk. I ran to Mother to ask where my new clothes were. She informed me that a family down the street had been completely burned out in a fire and needed clothing very badly. She said she realized the clothes were new, but that that family needed the clothes and she gave my new clothes to them.

I was very angry with Mother because I just couldn't understand why she couldn't have given them other clothes, that is older ones that were left in the closet. She said that one day I would understand why she did that. Well, I'm fifty-five years old and I still don't understand why she did that. Mother t-r-u-l-y had a generous and giving spirit. Maybe I should be embarrassed to say this, but even today, under the same circumstances, I still would not give my brand new clothes away. I would share other things I had and try to find others who could share also, but certainly not my new clothes.

Mother's encouragement. Mother enjoyed hearing me play the piano, and I always wanted to hear her tell me how good it sounded when I played any song. Many times I would be at the piano practicing my lessons and she would usually be in the kitchen finishing up with the dinner dishes. She would stop what she was doing, come into the living room, and prop her legs up on the coffee table to listen to me practice. I knew that I would be making many mistakes because the song was a new assignment that required a great deal of practice, so I requested that she wait until I had perfected the song before she listened to it. She would say, "Miss Ann, Mommy just loves to hear you play anything, even when you are practicing. You play so beautifully."

Mother would sometimes 'search me out' and ask me to play something pretty for her. This, of course, was exactly what I wanted to hear; this encouragement from Mother kept me playing the piano throughout high school and college. In later years when she heard Michelle and Erika play the piano, she told them they played the piano beautifully just like their mother. She encouraged them to keep practicing.

Memories of Daddy: Daddy always worked extra jobs so he wasn't around often. I recall one special incident that involved the purchase of a new refrigerator.

Many times Mother would need something for the house, and she hated to ask Daddy because he was so 'gruff' with her and her feelings were so easily hurt. I also felt that Mother should have stood up to Daddy more often than she did and I felt he should have been more understanding whenever she tried to talk to him. Since having children of my own, I now understand what Daddy's gruffness was about. It bothered him that Mother – or his children – had legitimate needs that were oftentimes difficult for him to fulfill because the money just wasn't available. It was not easy for him to say he didn't have the money. And, Mother didn't know how to ask for something and suggest some alternative solutions. Even if she did, I'm not sure he would have always given her time to share with him.

I had come home from college and the refrigerator had almost stopped keeping the food cold. Mother had to go to the store everyday to purchase just what she needed for that day and we had to eat it all up or it would spoil by the next day. Mother said she had told Daddy about the problem and he said he didn't have the money to buy a new refrigerator. I knew that Daddy had a revolving charge account at Sears so I took Mother to look at the type of refrigerator she felt she needed. We priced it and I talked to the credit department to find out how much greater the monthly bill would be if we purchased the refrigerator. Once I had gathered all the information, I sat down with Daddy and told him that I had checked everything out; I knew he could get the refrigerator for only a few additional dollars per month. He listened to me explain the idea and his face lit up. Then he told me to take Mother downtown and buy the refrigerator and have it delivered to the house. I tried to help Mother see how she could approach Daddy with possible solutions to meet her needs; however, she said that Daddy would listen to us better than he would to her. I knew this to be true because with Daddy it was necessary to be persistent. That was not Mother's nature.

Andrea C. Walker Ice, Senior Business Administrator, College of Evening and Continuing Education, University of Cincinnati

Kenneth, third son, eighth child

Where do I start? So many memories, so much love. I tear up just writing about them. My love for Mom and Dad is as fresh now as it has been since my knowledge of them. It is truly remarkable to have

176

had two such loving and caring parents. I thank God daily for the opportunity to have been born into the family of Anderson and Pauline Walker; in fact, I take a page out of Apostle Paul's writing when I say "I count it all a blessing" to have known and love them.

My most memorable moments of my days with Mom and Dad are many, but one incident stands out more clearly than some others. Daddy had told me to go down to the Laundromat (on Rat Row) and clean it up. When I arrived, there was only one lady there with two children; she was finishing up, folding her clothes. I immediately rushed to complete my cleaning so I could go and play basketball with Tom Jackson and the gang. After I finished, I did a 'no, no'. I left the Laundromat and went to the pool hall across the street. I was always able to get in because Curtis Smith and his brother, Jimmy ran the hall. During the day, they allowed school children to play on the back table – often for free. Well, on this day Curtis made a bet with a guy called Slim. The bet was that I could beat him if I was spotted (advanced) two balls. This meant that any two balls I wanted went off the table without penalty. Slim bet and I won. The problem was that many people had bet on that game. (To me, it was just an opportunity to play pool.)

After I won, Curtis's younger brother, Jimmy came up to me in anger. He had bet on Slim. Jimmy was speaking loudly and raving that the win was just luck, and I shouldn't be in the pool hall anyway. In an effort to provoke me, Jimmy brushed up against me and didn't say 'excuse me'. I brushed him back; this provoked a fight. We exchanged blows, then Curtis grabbed me from behind and pinned my arms while Jimmy hit me repeatedly. I managed to break loose, and I ran home to get Daddy's gun. I was hurt more about how things had happened than what had happened. I had not only won money for Curtis by beating Slim at pool, but I didn't ask Curtis to share with me. So, for him to hold my arms while his brother beat me was embarrassing. I ran into the house, got Daddy's twenty-two rifle and started out the house. Mama saw me with the rifle and called, "Kenny, where are you going with that rifle? What are you doing with it anyway?"

Crying, I paid no attention to her; I was running up Third Avenue. A short distance up the street, Willie Robinson, a classmate, met me. He saw what was happening and he tackled me and threw me into the ditch. As I lay there crying with embarrassment I saw Mama's shadow cover my head. She told me to get up, wipe my face and go into the house and stay there. She said she would have Daddy whip me when he got home. This was one of the longest days in my life: waiting for Daddy to come home and whip me. I had already received a whipping at the pool hall.

Now, I am looking forward to retirement and fishing and sunshine.

Kenneth O'Neal Walker, Systems Engineer, Lotus Notes Administrator, Spelman College, Atlanta, GA

George Walker is a cousin, who is like a brother.

Aunt Pauline: she could have set the pattern for the model housewife; she remained on the home front and raised her own children. She exhibited a most humble spirit to everyone in the community. Her spirit was visible in the Union Baptist Church Choir. She was a devoted Sunday school Teacher and she worked in leadership roles in church auxiliaries. These duties were performed religiously until her health declined. Aunt Pauline could be defined as a virtuous woman as characterized by the success and livelihoods of her children. She could have received the award for 'the print dress', which she wore on hot summer days. Aunt Pauline's attitude and humble spirit never changed; she was the same person whenever you met her.

Uncle Anderson set the mold as the model for a father and head of the household. He managed as if by systematic design the role of husband in his home. He provided in a way to raise his family, and he commanded his wife to remain at home with the children, and to give additional moral support to the home. Uncle Anderson managed to have his own transportation as a special asset to his family. After he retired from Swift Meatpacking Company, he founded his own taxi cab service. He was well organized and managed his business efficiently. It was necessary to retire from his business when his wife became ill. Uncle Anderson's life to his family was like a tree that was pruned to allow new growth. Certainly his family represents visible fruit in this millennium.

George Walker, Jr., City Councilman, Moultrie, GA.

One of my parents' sisters-in-law wanted to add some comments.

Anderson had a lot of influence in Moultrie. He was recognized highly. And he was good; he would help anybody he could. Pauline loved Anderson and he loved her. I knew them before they got married; we went to school together for a while.

Edna F. Hill, sister-in-law

A former sister-in-law, Opral Walker Davis added her statement:

I remember telling Daddy all about flying and how much fun it was; how I just loved it. His comments to me still makes me laugh: "If I am in my cab and I get a flat tire, I just pull over to the side of the road, get my jack out of the trunk and fix it. But if that plane gets a flat tire up in the air, ain't no fixin to be done. It is all over, Mr. Gentleman."
I can still hear Mama laughing and shaking her head, saying, "Walker, what kind of sense does that make?"
Daddy, by this time is shaking with laughter and trying to talk at the same time. We all know that this was not possible for Daddy.
Every time I fly – and I fly a lot- I think of Daddy and his first flight to Detroit to visit Uncle Jay.
My most precious memory of Daddy is sitting at the dinner table with him every evening smacking on Kentucky Fried Chicken and counting all his quarters from the day's runs in his cab. He and I would just talk and count money.
There are so many memories of Mama and our little private talks together. I remember literally begging her to have me a Blackberry Doobie ready whenever I would come to visit. She would always say, "You ol greedy girl", and just laugh, but the Blackberry Doobie would always be there waiting for me.
Whenever I see blackberries, I think of Mama's Blackberry Doobie.
My most memorable thought about a term that Mama would always make is this: She and I would be sitting on the porch and Daddy would fly by, she would say, "There goes your Daddy with one of his women." Or the telephone would ring, she would say, "That's one of your Daddy's women on the phone looking for him."
Needless to say, it took me a while to figure out what she meant. The first time I heard it, I thought, "How can Daddy be so bold?"

One day, during one of the many talks that Mama and I used to have, I told her my thoughts about her comments. Tears ran down her face as she nearly died of laughter. She laughed just as hard when I recounted it to Daddy.

Opral W. Davis, VP Products Operations Education Systems, Inc., La Jolla, CA

Adam Mattocks adopted Mama and Daddy as his second parents.

I arrived at Spence Air Base, Moultrie, Georgia in October 1957 for flight training. I was a newly appointed Second Lieutenant in the Air Force after obtaining my B.S. degree in Biological Science. I settled into my assigned B.O.Q. room to enter the first phase of my flight training (primary and basic training).

On Saturday, I drove into the town of Moultrie, Georgia and drove through the black section of town looking for a place to worship on Sunday. I was raised up in church and was a member of the First Baptist Church of Belgrade (Maysville, NC). I entered church Sunday morning and attended Sunday school and church as a visitor.

After worship service, members of the congregation graciously greeted me. Then a beautiful lady with a warm friendly smile, along with her husband, came up and introduced themselves as Mr. and Mrs. Walker. We talked for a minute or two and she asked where I was going since the worship service was over. I replied that I was going back to the base. Both of them said, "We are inviting you home for dinner." From that moment on I was never a stranger anymore, but I felt like family. This fellowship grew quickly into a binding friendship. They were my second set of parents.

It was not long before I began calling them Mom and Dad, and they called me A. C., their adopted son. They truly overflowed with love. (God is love). They had love and admiration for each other, love for their children, love for people, the church, the sick, and the community. I was a single man at that time living at Spence Air Base. They wanted me to spend weekends with them and their family, rather than at the base alone. They know I was the only black officer or military person at the base. I still admire their character and the personality they demonstrated to all. Later, I married Miss Annie Washington and they showed the same love for her as they did for me.

I remember the last time my wife and I stopped by to see them, Mom was very sick, and Dad was taking care of her. We all visited together for a while; then Mr. Walker (Dad) went into the kitchen to prepare something for Mrs. Walker (Mom). My wife and I stayed in the room for a while. Then I went into the kitchen where Dad was, and we talked a while. He informed me that Mom had been very, very sick, but was doing a little better now.

I thank God for them, and for providing me an opportunity to associate with them as part of their family. I pray that I sowed good things into them, for they have

Sowed many good things into me.

Adam Columbus Mattocks, Retired Officer, U. S. Air Force.

Four grandchildren also recorded their memories of Mama and Daddy.

Michael Holloway is one of Betty's children.

Besides our fishing trips and helping around the house, I don't remember anything that stuck with me. I do remember one thing that Granddaddy told me. I was scolding my son, and I said to him, "I'm going to break your neck!" Granddaddy said, "Michael, never tell a child you are going to break his neck when you know you don't mean it. The child knows you are not going to do it, so why say it."

Michael Holloway, Grandson

Margaret P. Hooker, my younger daughter

I'm sure there are many memories of Granddaddy and Grandmama, but this one stands out. One summer we were visiting our grandparents. One of the Holloways had received a walkie-talkie set. Granddaddy was really intrigued by it and wanted to try it out. Guess who agreed to be on the other end? Granddaddy, still working non-stop at that time, was also speaking VERY FAST. In addition, the walkie-talkies were not very sophisticated, so the static level was high. Granddaddy began talking and talking. I listened. I suppose he asked me a couple of questions, but I couldn't tell you anything about the conversation. Granddaddy continued speaking for a few minutes, and then walked back into the room that I was standing in. I'm sure he surmised what did/did not transpire because he began to laugh and patted me on the back (for my efforts, I suppose).

I just remember Granddaddy and Grandmama being there for summers we visited. I just took for granted that they were always around, even though I do not recall me or my siblings spending a great deal of time exclusively with them. Children take so many things for granted, including the adults in their lives.

As for Grandmama Pauline, my strongest memories of her, unfortunately, are of all the cooking! She seemed to deny us nothing, allowing any of us to go across the road to Mr. Miles' store if something we wanted was not available in the house. Just as we cleaned up after one meal it was time to begin preparing for the next. I do remember her fear of thunderstorms. She would insist that we unplug the TV, turn off the lights, not talk on the telephone, and sit very quietly until the storms passed. She was very adamant about this; it was one of the rare occasions she would chastise us if we did not immediately obey.

Margaret Pauline Hooker, Granddaughter

Melanie Hooker Johnson, my older daughter stated:

Grandma Pauline used to say, "We will all have to eat a little dirt before we die." I'm not sure why she said that; perhaps when I dropped my food and didn't want to eat it. But I think there was a deeper meaning there in terms of the sort of experiences we all have to endure if we live long enough. At least that's what I've come to see in that saying.

Granddaddy would always have something sweet to eat with dinner. I think that's where I picked up the habit (upside down smile).

A few other experiences I recall swinging on the front porch swing in the summers. I remember having to learn to say "Yes Mam" to my grandmother or maybe 'yes', but never 'yeah.' I remember people at the store or the washerteria perking up and showing deference when they learned that I (any of us) were 'Mr. Walker's grandchild (ren). I

182

remember an entire city of people having tremendous respect for my grandparents.

Melanie A. Hooker Johnson, Granddaughter

Darrell Walker Hooker, my youngest son

MONDAY CRICKETS

"Can you hear the Monday crickets, Granddaddy?"
"Naw I kan't! I got to run Miss Lady out over the way. I got crawlers, but the grasshoppers are all dead."
"Can you hear the Wednesday crickets, Granddaddy?"
"Naw, I got to be over to the church. Every Wednesday got to be to the church."
"Do you need some help with that?"
"Naw, you just watch yoself."

"Mom, Granddaddy lifted that boat all by himself!
"Can you hear the Friday crickets, Granddaddy?"
"Now Son, Friday's are my busy days. Folks get paid and I got to carry 'em all over."
"Can you hear the Saturday crickets, Granddaddy?"
"I believe I hear 'em a little. Dale, you going fishing with me and ya Grandmah?'
"Yes Sir!"
"Alligator? What's an alligator doing out here?"
"Dale, ain't it beautiful how the Lawd work?
He done made all these creatures you see flying and swimmin and crawlin
round here.
Now we bought them crickets from Mr. Man, and that's how he makes his livin to feed his people.
The fish tryin ta catch the crickets to eat dem and we tryin to catch the fish so we can eat them!
Ain't it som'in how God planned it all out that way?"

"Did you have a good Christmas, Granddaddy?"
"I jus sit here, me and ya grandmama, and thank God. He been so good to me.
Everyday like Christmas!"

"Can you hear the Monday crickets, Granddaddy?"

"Good gracious alive, Son! You know they sound just as pretty as they wonna be."

"Ain't it som'in Granddaddy!
Ain't it som'in how God planned it out that way!"

Darrell Walker Hooker, Manager, Maggiano's "Little Italy" Restaurant Atlanta, GA

**Daddy's favorite
leisure activity was fishing.
ncle J.T and Daddy show their catch.**

Daddy and grandson, Darrell Hooker
pose with the catch for dinner

Daddy was proud of his self-employed
status. He had his taxicab business for
25 years

Son-in-law Mose Ensley
with Mama & Daddy
1984

Mama posed for a
sassy picture
1984

Epilogue

I began to write this book as a module of my Ph.D. program. In March 2000, there seemed to be no more challenges in my life. My children were all successfully launched in their careers and I was gainfully employed, but something was lacking. One of the things I thought I had always wanted to do was earn a Ph.D. When I shared with my children that I was going back to school, my daughters, Melanie, and Margaret quit their jobs and returned to school.

Melanie enrolled in Columbia College in Chicago to study film and television writing. She completed her internship at HBO in Hollywood. The experience was challenging; money was always in short supply. She stayed on in Los Angeles for six months, but found no work. She returned to Cincinnati, Ohio in August 2002. She was hired as Information Technology Program Coordinator, and she is teaching at the University of Cincinnati, Adjunct Faculty

Margaret enrolled in the Culinary Institute of America in Hyde Park, New York. She completed her externship in Atlanta and stayed on to live and work there. Margaret still exhibits Grandmama Pauline's caring spirit: she remembers every family member's birthday every year with a suitable greeting card. She and David share his home.

David also returned to school; he is studying theology at Emory University. He arranges his work to fall on weekends, and occasionally travels to third world countries to work. His professors cooperate with his work efforts; often, he can coordinate his work with his class requirements. Last September (2002) he worked in Nigeria for three weeks, teaching grassroots organizing, conflict resolutions, and mediation techniques. When he returned to Atlanta, his presence was requested by a group of people who are trying to organize conflict transformation. They say that there is no satisfactory solution to conflicts; what is necessary is transformation. Thus, the new terminology, "conflict transformation." He plans to study with them again next summer (2003). In March 2003 he plans to travel to Cuba as part of a class assignment.

Douglas and Patrise became grandparents in 2001. Doug recently completed writing a symphony he began in 1992. He continues his work with the engineering consulting firm as V.P. and is also actively involved in civic and community affairs. Patrise ran for elective office in 2000. She finished second in the race for district commissioner. She has returned to her law practice and continues active involvement in community affairs.

Darrell is a restaurant manager in Atlanta. He hopes to be promoted and relocated to North Carolina this year. In February, he and McKenna came to visit me for two days. He came to help me buy a new car. I was impressed with his skills with salesmen. He understands car salesmanship well because he once worked as an automobile salesman. He told me he intends to return to school to become a real estate evaluator. He needs a second job because he wants LaTonya to remain at home with McKenna until she starts school.

Homer (Randy) lives in Memphis, TN. He has retired as a hospital administrator, and now works as a hospital management consultant.

My children have all shown much courage in their growing up; after all, to change careers in mid-stream requires faith and courage. As Dr. Martin Luther King, Jr. said,
"Courage faces fear and thereby masters it. Cowardice represses fear and is thereby mastered by it.
Courageous men never lose their zest for living even though their life situation is zestless; cowardly men, overwhelmed by the uncertainties of life, lose the will to live.
We must constantly build dykes of courage to hold back the flood of fear."

Twenty-eight months into my Ph.D. program, I withdrew from the University. With no end goal in mind, I asked God to guide me about pursuing this difficult path. It was getting to be burdensome financially and time consuming and emotionally draining. The answer to my prayer came in one of my daily devotional readings. The Scripture was Philippians 2: 1-11. When I read verse three, the words jumped out at me. "Do nothing out of selfish ambition and vain conceit, ..." That was the answer I had prayed for. Next, I prayed for the courage to confront myself. With courage granted, and without further thought, I completed and mailed my official withdrawal form to Union Institute and University and my Core Advisor.

Many people protested my decision, but I knew it was the right one. On July 4, 2002, I felt FREE!

I shall continue the projects I started: writing this book, publishing the interviews with courageous overcomers, and continuing The Great Black Books Reading Clubs. This whole experience has confirmed a conviction I hold: Children do what you DO, not what you SAY. I thank God for making me a role model to my children.

If Daddy and Mama had lived to witness our next family reunion, they would have marveled at how many of their children and grandchildren fulfilled their desire to see us educated. Six of my siblings and I hold post secondary degrees, some of us earned post-graduate degrees. Our children collectively have done equally well. We can boast of a doctor, a nurse, two lawyers, an engineer, a financial analyst, four computer technicians, a college teacher, a journalist, several educators and on and on. We keep striving with heads held high, demonstrating the legacy of my southern parents.

##